JOKING APART

A Play

ALAN AYCKBOURN

CW00553074

SAMUEL FRENCH

FRENCH

LONDON
NEW YORK SYDNEY TORONTO HOLLYWOOD

JOKING APART

First presented at the Stephen Joseph Theatre, Scarborough, on January 11th, 1978, and subsequently in London by Michael Codron at the Globe Theatre on the 7th March 1979, with the following cast of characters:

Richard	Christopher Cazenove
Anthea	Alison Steadman
Hugh	Julian Fellowes
Louise	Marcia Warren
Sven	Robert Austin
Olive	Jennifer Piercey
Brian	John Price
Melody	
Mandy	Diane Bull
Mo	
Debbie	

The play directed by ALAN AYCKBOURN

Setting by Alan Tagg

The action takes place in the garden of Richard's and Anthea's house

Act I	Scene 1	Twelve years ago, 5th November, 7.15 p.m.
	Scene 2	Eight years ago, July morning, Sunday
Act II	Scene 1	Four years ago, Boxing Day, 3.00 p.m.
	Scene 2	This year, August evening, Friday

ACT I

SCENE 1

A Garden, about 7.15 p.m. on November 5th, twelve years ago

Part of a tennis court can be seen; although in disrepair underfoot, it has solid enough fencing and the door is in working order. The rest of the court extends off stage. At the other side is a small summerhouse/pavilion, very weathered. There is rough grass underfoot, together with bushes and trees. A wonderful garden for children, slightly more hazardous for adults

At present it is dark, a fine clear night, with a little moon. From the other side of the tennis court comes the sound of three children's (aged between four and six) excited shrieks and yelps

> *Richard, a man in his late twenties, enters from the far end of the tennis court. He has on suitable bonfire gear—scarf, coat, old trousers and gumboots, thick gloves and possibly a hat. He carries a battery lantern*

Richard (*shouting to the children behind him*) Now, the first one of you to touch those fireworks goes up on the bonfire instead of the guy, all right? Now, Debbie, you're the oldest. I'm leaving you in charge, young lady.

Anthea (*off from the house*) Are we all ready?

Richard Oh, come on, you lot. We've been waiting out here for hours.

Anthea (*off*) Coming.

Richard Have you brought the matches?

Anthea (*off*) Brian's bringing them.

> *Anthea appears, a year or two younger than Richard: cheerful, disarmingly frank, attractive but not beautiful*

God, this place is treacherous in the dark. (*Extending her hand to someone behind her*) Do be careful, Mrs—er—Emerson. Can you see? (*She waves a small pocket torch which she is carrying ineffectually*)

Richard (*bounding forward with his larger lantern*) Here, let me ...

> *It can now be seen that Anthea is leading the Emersons: Louise, a pale, rather tense woman of twenty-four and Hugh, her husband a young clergyman, two years older. Shy, rather nervous but with an air of quiet determination*

Louise That's fine, thank you. I can manage.

Hugh (*in the dark*) Ahhh ...

Richard All right back there?

Hugh Yes, thank you, Mr Clarke.

Anthea (*moving towards the summerhouse*) We're going to watch over here, darling, if that's all right?

Richard You're a bit far away. You won't see much from there.
Anthea No, this is fine.
Richard Come in the tennis court.
Anthea No. Mrs Emerson doesn't like the bangs, darling.
Richard We haven't got many bangs. She wouldn't let me buy many bangs. Bangs are the best bit.
Anthea No, we're happy. Mrs Emerson and I will be perfect here.
Louise Please do call me Louise.
Anthea Oh fine. In that case, I'm Anthea. This is Richard.
Richard How do you do?
Hugh Hugh.
Richard I beg your pardon?
Hugh I'm Hugh.
Richard You're what? Oh Hugh, I see. Hallo. Right. I'll set things going. Where's Brian with the matches?
Anthea (*calling*) Brian!
Richard Brian!
Anthea Brian!
Richard We're not waiting for the Holmensons, are we?
Anthea No, they're obviously going to be late.
Richard Late? Late? Sven is never late. You must know that by now. Everyone else has got to be early. (*Shouting*) Brian!

Richard goes off towards the house

Anthea (*laughing*) This is Richard's partner and his wife. Sven and Olive Holmenson. Sven is terribly solemn, terribly Scandinavian, a sweet person but never, ever wrong.
Louise Really?
Hugh How awfully convenient.
Louise I can't believe that. I mean, nobody ...
Anthea Well, he never admits he's wrong. Let's put it that way. I mean, you could go up to him and say, "Excuse me, Sven, I'm afraid you're on fire. Your jacket is alight and blazing." And he'll say, "No, no, I'm not," and that's the end of it. No point in arguing.
Louise When was this?
Anthea What?
Louise The ...
Anthea Oh, no, sorry. I've got fire on the brain with this bonfire. That was just a sort of example. I mean, that sort of thing.
Hugh He wasn't really on fire, dear.
Louise Oh. That's a relief.
Anthea No, you'll have to get used to me. I chat away sixteen to the dozen. Nobody knows what I'm talking about, least of all myself. Not that anybody cares. Most of the time nobody's listening anyway.
Hugh It's really very kind of you to ask us.
Anthea Well, you'll be feeling a bit stranded, won't you? I mean, how long have you been moved in? A couple of days, isn't it?
Louise Yes, two days. Literally.

During the following, Hugh sidles away from them and down the side of the tennis court to check on his offspring

Anthea You got everything straight yet?
Louise No, I'm afraid not. It's a terrible mess, I'm glad to be able to shut the door on it for ten minutes.
Anthea Well, we've been here six months and our place is just chaos.
Louise Of course you're in a very big house, aren't you?
Anthea Enormous.
Hugh (*crouching down and talking through the wire mesh*) All right, Christopher? Now, be a good boy. Play nicely with the little girl and boy, won't you?

During the above Richard returns with the matches

Anthea Got them?
Richard Yes.
Louise Is he all right, dear?
Hugh Yes. He's getting a tiny bit over-excited, I think.
Richard (*calling*) All right, kids, just a second.
Anthea Aren't Brian and thingy coming out?
Richard I don't know. (*Pulling a face*) Things are a bit tense in there.
Anthea Oh.
Richard I thought I'd better leave them. (*Moving into the tennis court*) Now then, you 'orrible lot. What's been going on behind here?

Richard goes

Anthea (*to Hugh and Louise*) Brian, whom you met and girl-friend whom you haven't. Going through agonies all weekend.
Louise Oh dear.
Anthea Ah well, that's love. I suppose.
Hugh Yes, yes.
Louise It's very good for our Christopher to have some other children to play with.
Anthea Didn't he have any friends before?
Louise No, there weren't any his own age where we were.
Anthea Oh dear. How old is he?
Louise Four-and-a-half.
Anthea Oh well, he's just between ours. Debbie's, what, nearly six and Giles was four last Thursday.
Richard (*off*) Here we go then. Ready?
Anthea Right.
Louise (*covering her ears and shutting her eyes*) Oh.

There is the blaze of a firework

Anthea Whee! Isn't that pretty?
Hugh (*trying to make his wife hear him*) It's all right, Louise, it's all right.
Anthea (*amused*) Is she all right?
Hugh She doesn't like the bangs.

Anthea There aren't any bangs. Tell her we haven't got any bangs.
Hugh (*shouting*) They haven't got any bangers, Louise.

A second different coloured firework goes off, with cries from the children

Anthea Darling? Richard?
Richard Hallo?
Anthea If you're going to light a bang, could you give us some warning so it doesn't frighten Louise.
Richard (*off*) I'll try.
Anthea We're bringing some food out later on when we've lit the bonfire.
Hugh Lighting it in the middle of the tennis court, is that a good idea? I mean, it won't do it a lot of good, will it?
Anthea No, well with that court, it doesn't matter that much.

Another firework goes off. Louise, who has emerged temporarily from her shell, goes back into it again

It's in a terrible state. We're going to have to have it redone sometime. I don't think the previous owners ever used it. Do you play, either of you? (*Looking towards Louise*) Oh. (*She sees she will get no answer from that quarter*)
Hugh (*answering for them both*) I do a little. But I don't think Louise does.
Anthea Well, I'm hopeless. We must learn together.
Hugh Good idea.

The firework light goes out

Louise (*emerging*) All clear?
Anthea Yes, all clear now.

A big bang. Louise screams and covers her ears. Hugh moves back down the side of the tennis court to check on his offspring

Richard (*off*) Sorry. That was a banger.
Anthea Thank you, darling.
Hugh (*crouching down by the side of the wire*) Christopher? Keep your bala-clava on, there's a good boy. You keep your little hat on, there's a good boy.
Louise I am sorry. They just make me jump, I can't ...
Anthea That's all right. It was frightfully loud. No, what I was going to say was, our house, of course, was the original vicarage. Did you know that ...

A firework screams overhead. Louise ducks

And then, of course, they built—oh lord ... (*calling*) Richard, have you got any quieter ones? Poor Louise is cowering away here.
Richard (*off*) Sorry.
Hugh (*hurrying back*) Yes, I'm sorry. She shouldn't really have come. She's absolutely terrified of bangers.
Anthea Would you like to wait in the house?
Richard (*off, to one of the children*) Oy, oy, oy. Hands off.

Hugh hurries off to investigate

Louise No, I'm fine, fine.

Hugh Is Christopher being a nuisance—er—Richard? Shall I take him?

Richard (*off*) No, he's all right. Just a bit over-excited ... (*Suddenly, fiercely*) Giles, that is still alight. Now put it down.

Hugh (*off*) Now, Christopher, quieten down. Quieten down, dear.

During the above, Brian, a man in his late twenties appears from the house. He stands moodily apart

Anthea (*spotting Brian*) Oh come on, Brian, you're missing it all. Is Melody coming out?

Brian I have no idea whatsoever.

Anthea Where is she?

Brian In the kitchen, I think, heating the soup.

Another brilliantly coloured firework

Anthea Oh, good for her. (*Taking in the firework*) I say, what a gorgeous colour. What's this one called, darling?

Brian wanders away and gazes morosely at the display without enjoyment. Hugh sidles after him

Richard (*off*) I haven't the faintest idea.

Anthea (*calling*) Giles, look at the colours. Giles? Honestly, the kid's half-witted. He's looking in the wrong direction. Turn him round, Debbie, so he can see. Brian's working for Richard. Just temporarily. He's working in the retail shop. We import a lot of household stuff. Glassware—furniture—fabrics and so on. From Scandinavia.

Louise Ah.

Hugh (*to Brian*) Mild enough, anyway.

Brian Yeah.

There is a silence between them

Anthea Are you glad you're here? I mean, is this the sort of parish you wanted?

Louise Well, yes. Of course, it is only our first proper parish. We were very lucky to get it at all. I'm delighted. I think Hugh wanted more of an urban area but I love the country, you see. I was brought up in the country ...

A firework blazes. Louise blocks her ears. Anthea absent-mindedly follows suit

(*continuing loudly*) It'll be a challenge. Our predecessor, the Reverend Armthwaite, he was here for fifteen years. He was very popular.

Anthea (*unhearing*) Yes, yes.

Louise So we have a lot to live up to, I'm afraid.

Anthea No, no, quite.

A swoosh of a rocket

Oh look, a rocket.

Richard (*off*) Rocket just gone up.

Anthea Yes.

Hugh (*to Brian*) Rocket.

Brian Yes.

Hugh Do you live locally?

Brian No.

Hugh Ah.

Brian I'm just here for the week-end.

Hugh I see. Friend of the family?

Brian Something like that.

Anthea Watch the rocket, children. See? No, up, Giles. Up. It's up there, you fool. Honestly.

Louise Of course, in a way, I mean, I know your house is much more historical and interesting but I think in some ways, I prefer our little new house. I mean, as far as day to day running is concerned.

Anthea Oh gosh, yes, yours any day.

Louise I mean, it should be very easy to keep up. I don't normally like red-brick that much but I don't find, in this case, it's obtrusive at all. And as for keeping it clean...

Anthea Oh, there's no comparison. None at all. Modern houses are wonderful for that. I mean, we only got this place because it was going for absolutely nothing. And we happened to know the previous owner, that sort of thing. We wouldn't have bought it otherwise.

Louise It must be very difficult to keep clean.

Anthea It must be. I never tried. The place is a tip. Fortunately none of my family seems to mind. They're a totally squalid bunch.

Louise Oh.

Richard (*off*) This is an Arctic Snowstorm.

Anthea What?

Richard (*off*) It's called an *Arctic Snowstorm*.

Anthea Lovely. Darling, can you make sure Giles sees this one. I mean, you've set fire to a fortune out there and he's seen absolutely none of it. Debbie, don't pick noses with gloves on, please.

Louise No, I think we're going to find this job a very stimulating and challenging one. I'm really looking forward to it. And Hugh's full of good ideas. He's absolutely bursting with them. What he wants to do—

Anthea Golly! Sorry to interrupt you but just look at this. Isn't it lovely?

Louise (*covering her ears*) Oh yes.

Richard (*off*) What about that?

Anthea (*moving towards the tennis court*) It's almost like daylight. It's—good God! What on earth is your little boy doing by the fireworks? Richard, Richard, stop him.

Richard (*off*) Oh, my God...

Hugh Christopher. Christopher, you naughty boy. Stop that.

Louise (*simultaneously*) Christopher, Christopher, you little beast. Hugh, stop him.

Richard (*off simultaneously*) Oy, oy, oy.

Hugh You naughty boy. You naughty, naughty boy.

Hugh goes into the court and disappears. Louise follows him

Louise Right, Christopher, I'm taking you straight home. I'm taking you straight home this minute. I'm taking him home, Hugh ...

Hugh (*off*) You hear that, Christopher. Mummy's taking you home.

During the above, Brian goes back towards the house. Richard comes into sight in the tennis court, abandoning the Emersons to their offspring, and shrugs towards Anthea

Anthea Yes, that's right, Giles. Christopher did a wee-wee in the fireworks. Wasn't that funny? Giles thinks it's a hoot.

Richard Oh well, on to the bonfire.

Anthea (*calling*) It's all right, Debbie, don't cry now. Daddy's going to light the bonfire.

Hugh (*off*) Naughty boy ...

Lousie (*off*) Naughty, naughty boy ...

Richard Don't worry, Hugh, don't worry about it.

Hugh reappears

Hugh I am so sorry. I don't know what to say.

Richard No need.

Anthea Light the bonfire, darling.

Richard Coming up.

Richard goes off through the tennis court

Hugh (*approaching Anthea*) I am absolutely mortified. I don't know how to apologize.

Anthea It's just the excitement.

Hugh He's suddenly started behaving like this. It's most weird.

Anthea Does he do a lot of that sort of thing?

Hugh No, not that particularly. But he suddenly gets these furious rages.

Louise appears momentarily on the tennis court

Louise I'm taking him home.

Hugh All right. I'll follow you.

Louise Don't be too long. He won't go to sleep unless you're there.

Hugh All right. Five minutes, I promise.

Louise (*to Anthea*) May I go back this way?

Anthea Yes, do. Just squeeze through the gap. (*Calling*) Richard. Could you hold the fence for them so they can get through the gap?

Louise goes

Richard (*off*) Right.

Louise (*off*) Come along, you naughty little boy.

Anthea By the way, it goes without saying, I hope, but do feel free, any of you, or your friends to use this garden when you want to.

Hugh That's really most ...

Anthea They've been a bit stingy with your garden, haven't they? You haven't got much, have you?

Hugh No, not—er ...

Anthea They just pinched enough of this garden to build your house and left
it at that. Still, you've got nothing to mow or cut or prune—I suppose you
can look on the bright side ...

Hugh I still don't know how to apologize ...

*Brian enters. He carries a tray with soup mugs and a dish of hot sausages.
Melody, a woman of about Brian's age, follows him*

Brian Soup. (*He puts the tray on the summerhouse table*)

Anthea Oh, well done. Hallo, Melody.

Melody Hallo.

Brian Sausages.

Anthea Melody, this is Hugh.

Melody Hallo.

Anthea Hugh's our new vicar. Just moved into the house at the bottom of
the garden. Melody's from Canada. She's a friend of Brian's.

Melody You want soup?

Hugh Oh, thank you.

Melody You're welcome. (*She pours soup*)

Brian Shall I take some round to Richard?

Hugh Oh no, let me please. Let me do something to make up.

Melody (*handing soup to Hugh*) That's yours.

Hugh Thank you.

Anthea Have a sausage as well.

Hugh Oh well, wouldn't say no.

Melody (*handing Hugh a second cup*) That's for Richard.

Hugh Oh, thank you.

Melody You're welcome.

*Hugh moves away, laden with sausages and two mugs of soup. He goes into
the tennis court*

(*Pouring another cup*) That's yours.

Anthea Thank you.

Melody You want some, lover boy?

Brian Yes.

The bonfire crackles alight with a roar

Richard (*off*) There she goes. Watch yourself, Hugh.

Anthea Hooray! (*Tasting soup*) This has turned out quite well.

Melody The sausages are there. (*She stomps off towards the bonfire*)

Anthea Where are you going?

Melody I don't want to be in the way.

Melody exits

Brian Oh God.

Anthea Did I say something I shouldn't?

Brian Oh forget it, forget it.

Anthea What?

Brian Forget it. Forget her. I'm sorry for bringing her down. I might have known.

Anthea She was very jolly yesterday.

Brian Oh, she can be if it suits her.

Anthea Oh Brian, try not to argue all week-end, there's a love. I mean, we adore you coming down here but you always seem to bring down some girl you loathe the sight of and then shout at her all week-end.

Brian And why do you think that is?

Anthea Well, can't you find one you like?

Brian gives a bitter laugh

Richard (*off*) There goes the guy.

Anthea Oh, super. Hooray! (*Sotto voce again*) What do you mean?

Brian Are you that naïve?

Anthea What?

Brian Do you really think that because you're living with Richard my feelings for you have changed one iota? Do you?

Melody enters

Anthea Oh Brian, come on.

Brian (*gripping her arm*) Well, do you?

Anthea Oh, for heaven's sake ...

Melody watches them, amused

Melody Go ahead.

Anthea (*pulling away*) Oh, don't be ridiculous. Do be your age, Brian.

Anthea goes up the side of the tennis court and disappears

Brian (*glaring at Melody*) Enjoying yourself?

Melody Get lost.

Brian (*going towards the house*) Don't stand too close to the fire, you'll melt.

Melody (*screaming after him*) Aw, screw you, brother! Screw you!

Brian goes. Simultaneously, Hugh appears round the other side of the bonfire. He stands next to Melody

Hugh (*conversationally*) Warm enough here. (*Pause*) Of course, you won't have Guy Fawkes' Day in Canada, will you? (*Pause*) No. It's very beautiful, I understand. So I've read. Of course in the south, you have the great lakes and, of course, the Niagara Falls. Then you have the big wheat-growing districts. Alberta. Manitoba. Saskatchewan. And then further north, you have the North-West Territories, of course. And a whole mass of lakes. Not forgetting good old Baffin Island.

Melody Why are you telling me this?

Hugh I beg your pardon?

Melody I don't want to hear all this. I know all this. I come from the god-damned place.

Hugh Ah.

Melody I don't want to hear about it. Why do you think I'm here?

Hugh Ah.

Melody Because I hated the place.

Hugh I'm sorry, I was ... (*He moves away unhappily*)

Melody (*calling after him*) Reverend?

Hugh Mmm?

Melody I'm sorry. That was rude. That was churlish. That was ungracious. Will you accept my apology?

Hugh Er, well. Yes.

Melody I think I would like you to understand. You see that dummy? That thing burning up there? That poor little helpless, half-charred rag doll?

Hugh The guy.

Melody The guy? You call that the guy? Well, I'm like that guy, Reverend. Do you understand that? Someone is trying to burn me alive.

Hugh Metaphorically, I take it?

Melody Metaphorically. Any other phorically. You name it. He uses me like a pawn in some game he's playing with that woman. My God, he has tried to take away my dignity. How dare he take away my dignity. Jesus Christ. I'm sorry, I'm sorry. God bless you, Reverend, God bless you and keep you. Why should you care about my problems?

Melody hurries off towards the house.

Hugh stands perplexed

Richard comes round the other side of the bonfire

Richard (*as he enters*) Watch Giles, Debbie, just for a minute. Don't let him get any closer. Now then, Hugh, are you being looked after?

Hugh Oh yes ...

Richard Where is everyone?

Hugh Well, I'm not ... I think ...

Richard (*calling*) Anthea. Antie.

Anthea (*off, beyond the tennis court*) Hallo.

Richard Now, what can I get you? More soup?

Hugh I really ought to be getting back.

Richard Oh, go on, please. Sven hasn't turned up, we've got far too much. What have we got here? Aha, sausages. Have some of these.

Hugh Thank you ... (*He helps himself to one*)

Richard Go on, go on. Take a handful.

Hugh (*complying*) Well ...

Richard (*as he pours the soup for them*) No, though I say it myself when it comes to soups, Anthea takes a lot of beating.

Hugh Yes. I don't actually usually drink it but this is really quite ...

Richard Oh, she knows her soups.

Hugh (*taking his mug*) Thank you. Yes, I must say I rather envy you. I—er—Louise doesn't claim to be anything of a cook so I'm not being disloyal. She really doesn't see eye to eye with a stove at all.

Richard Oh dear. What about you?

Hugh Me?

Richard Do you cook?

Hugh No. Not at all.
Richard You should learn. Highly satisfying. I always cook at the week-ends. It's very relaxing.

Anthea enters

Anthea They're having a wonderful display over in the distance there. Dozens of rockets. Are the kids all right?
Richard I'm going back. I'm just feeding up Hugh. He claims his wife starves him. (*He surveys the bonfire*)
Anthea No.
Hugh No, I didn't say that. I ...
Anthea Grief. He's eating sausages by the fistful.
Hugh I'm sorry.
Anthea No, please do, there's masses. I'm joking. Please (*She smiles dazzlingly at Hugh*)

Hugh manages to smile limply back

Richard That's burning really well this year. I think I've found the knack of building them ...
Hugh Wonderful.
Anthea I've just been having a snoop up at the end there. You know, Richard, it wouldn't be a huge job to widen that gap in their fence and put a sort of gate there. And then Hugh and Louise could use the garden whenever they wanted.
Richard Why don't we knock the whole fence down altogether and have done with it? Ridiculous putting a fence there anyway. Not even well-designed. If we took it down, they could look out at the garden instead of a fence.
Anthea What a marvellous idea. (*To Hugh*) Don't you agree?
Hugh Well, it's—yes—I mean ...
Anthea Come on, let's knock it down.
Richard I'll do it now. Why not?
Hugh Now?
Richard Burn it on the bonfire. Best way ...

Richard goes off above the tennis court

Hugh Well, I ...
Anthea There you are. No sooner said than done ... (*yelling*) Check the kids.
Richard (*off*) Right.
Hugh Well, I hope Louise is agreeable.
Anthea Heavens, she'd far sooner look at trees than a fence. Besides this was your garden originally.
Hugh Well, yes.

She smiles at him again. He smiles back

Anthea Look, we're not actually church-going people or anything, you know—either of us—but if there's anything we can do to help—you know, organizing or just fetching and carrying, do ask us, won't you? We'd be only too pleased.

Hugh Well, that is kind. Thank you.
Anthea We're always here.

There is a distant splintering of timber, and a gleeful yell from Richard

Heavens, what is he doing?
Hugh Yes. Well, we might actually call on you sooner than you ...

Anthea offers him another sausage

Thank you ... sooner than you think. I think, especially early on, we're going
to need all the help we can get. I mean, I really intend to get involved in
as many different spheres as possible. My predecessor was, well, fairly
ancient and—understandably, I think—he let things slide a bit. I noticed
the other Sunday when I visited, there were very few young people in evi-
dence. I'm hoping to remedy that ...

Another splintering crash, and yell from Richard

I hope your husband knows what he's doing. He'll stop when he gets to
our house, will he? That's not to say that I want to discourage older people.
Of course not. But it's a bit depressing if most of your congregation are
in the churchyard instead of the church. (*He laughs*)

Richard enters brandishing a piece of timber

Richard Piece of cake. The most pathetic fence I've ever come across.
Anthea Don't go too mad, darling.
Richard Trust me.

Richard goes

Hugh I must say, when your husband does a job, he certainly ...
Anthea Hugh, I'm going to have to correct you on one thing.
Hugh Yes?
Anthea I'm afraid Richard's not my husband. We're not married.
Hugh Oh.
Anthea Oh gosh. You're not shocked, are you? You're not going to go all
Church Militant on me?
Hugh No, no, not at all. Not these days, no. Are the children ...?
Anthea They're my children. They're not Richard's. I'm divorced from my
first husband whose children they are. Richard is separated from his first
wife who has no children.
Hugh I see. I see. Are you known as Mrs Clarke?
Anthea I couldn't honestly care less. Everyone calls me Anthea. But Mrs
Clarke if you like or even Mrs Watkins or if you really insist Miss Braddles-
tone. Though I'm not too fond of that one which is why I got married.
Hugh Ah well. If you ever want to—if you're ever in a position to make it
official, I'd be glad if you came to us first.
Anthea (*offering him a sausage*) But we'd be divorced. Doesn't that ...?
Hugh (*accepting*) Oh, we're not so fussy these days. Glad of the trade. I'm
sorry, I'm eating all these.
Anthea Go ahead.

Hugh Not so much the Church Militant as the Church Ravenous. (*He laughs awkwardly*)

Louise (*off, distant*) Hugh. Hugh.

Hugh stops laughing

Anthea Was that someone?

Louise (*off*) Hugh, where are you?

Hugh It's Louise.

Anthea Oh.

Louise enters from the direction of the house

Louise Hugh? What are you doing?

Hugh What?

Louise Where have you been?

Hugh Here. I've been here.

Louise But I thought you said ...

Anthea Is anything wrong?

Louise There's someone round the back of the house breaking down our fence. They're just ripping it down. I looked out of the bathroom window. They're kicking at it. Pulling it away in chunks.

Hugh Ah yes, well. That'll be Richard.

Louise Who?

Hugh Mr Clarke. Richard—he's ...

Anthea Oh dear ...

Louise Richard? You mean, Mr ...? Why is he doing it?

Hugh Well, I said he could.

Louise You said he could knock down our fence?

Hugh We thought it might be nicer.

Louise Why?

Hugh Er ...

Anthea I think it's probably my fault—well, our fault. We thought it'd be rather nice for you to use the whole garden, that's all.

Louise But this is your garden.

Anthea Well, yes but ...

Louise Our garden was on the other side of that fence.

Anthea Yes.

Louise When there was a fence. Now we haven't got a fence so we haven't got a garden at all.

Hugh Well, we've got this garden.

Louise No, this is their garden. I'm talking about our garden. I don't want their garden. I want our garden.

An ear-splitting crash

Richard (*off, distant*) Whey-hey!

Hugh I'm sorry—I ...

Anthea (*calling*) Richard! Richard, could you stop a minute, darling?

Richard What's that?

Anthea I said, could you stop ... (*She moves off towards him*)

Richard (*off, distant*) Yes, all right. All finished now.
Anthea Richard.

Anthea goes off past the tennis court

Hugh (*smiling faintly*) Have you left Christopher?
Louise Yes, he's in bed.
Hugh Right. I'll ... (*He takes a swig of his soup*)
Louise What's that you're drinking?
Hugh Oh. Just soup. Some home-made soup.
Louise You don't like soup.
Hugh Well, not usually.
Louise How come you suddenly like soup?
Hugh Yes, well, we better just say good night and—um ...
Louise I think it's terrible. Just pulling down somebody's fence like that. Without even asking them. I mean, it wasn't even their fence. It was our fence. I don't feel secure without that fence. Anybody could walk into that garden. Anyone could look in through the windows.
Hugh Well, I'll get another. I'm sorry.

Richard and Anthea creep on, rather sheepishly

Oh, good night, Richard.
Richard I hear we might have been a bit premature.
Hugh Yes.
Richard Sorry.
Louise You coming, Hugh?
Hugh Yes.
Louise Hurry up then. He won't go to sleep without you.

Louise goes out to the house

Hugh I'm sorry. This was my fault.
Anthea Is she frightfully upset?
Hugh She'll be all right. She has these little tempers. But they're nothing ...
Anthea Would you like to take her some soup?
Hugh No. No, thank you. Anyway, I've had a very pleasant evening and I'm so pleased we're neighbours and—er—so on. I look forward to seeing a lot of you. Good night.
Sven (*off*) Hallo? Where is everyone? Hallo?
Anthea It's Sven! You must meet Sven and Olive, Hugh.
Richard (*calling*) Sven.
Hugh Well, I ...

Sven enters. He is thirty, already trying hard to be fifty. There is a great sense of importance about him

Anthea Sven.
Sven Anthea, my darling, my darling. (*He holds out his arms*)
Anthea Oh Sven.

Sven and Anthea embrace

Olive, twenty-eight—already rather staid—enters

Olive Hallo, Richard.

Richard How's lovely Olive?

Anthea This is ridiculous. It's as if we haven't seen them for months.

Sven Six weeks... Hallo, Richard. How are you? Six weeks we've been away.

Anthea Hallo, Olive.

Olive Oh, Anthea, I really could kill you. I could throttle you, girl, look at you. You've got thinner.

Anthea I haven't.

Olive How dare you get thinner? It isn't fair. It really isn't. I wouldn't mind but she never stops eating.

Richard Olive, Sven. Can we introduce Hugh? The Reverend Hugh Emerson. He's now living at the cottage at the bottom there.

Olive What, the little red-brick Wendy house? That's nice.

Richard This is Olive Holmenson.

Olive How do you do?

Hugh How do you do?

Richard And Sven Holmenson.

Hugh How do you do?

Sven So? You've chosen to live next door to these crazy people, eh?

Hugh Yes, yes ...

Sven God help you. But in your case, he probably will. Now then, where are these fireworks?

Anthea We've had them.

Sven Had them?

Richard (*gesticulating to Anthea*) Kids.

Richard moves back to the bonfire

Anthea You're an hour late.

Sven Late? Who's late? (*Holding out his watch*) Look at this. Half-past eight. Dead on time.

Anthea We said half-past seven. We wouldn't have said ...

Sven Anthea, Anthea. Half-past eight. Believe me, that's what you said. Half-past eight.

Anthea Oh well, it doesn't matter. Let's take you in.

Olive Yes, I must have a wash.

Sven If you had said half-past seven, my darling, I would have been here at half-past seven.

Anthea (*calling to Richard*) Are they okay?

Sven But as you said half-past eight, we've come at half-past eight.

Anthea Oh Sven, you really are impossible.

Olive He's never wrong about times. Sven's never wrong where time's concerned.

Sven It's true. Never about times.

Anthea Can I take that for you, Olive?

Olive Oh, it's not heavy. I've got a couple of little things for the kiddies. And I've brought some of that Danish chocolate you like.

Olive exits

Anthea Oh, you shouldn't. You staying for a drink, Hugh?
Hugh Oh, no, no ...
Anthea Good night then.
Hugh Good night.
Olive (*now far in the distance*) Good night.
Richard (*who is playing 'monsters' with the kids*) Arrghhh...!

Anthea goes off after Olive

Hugh (*calling to Richard on the far side of the tennis court*) Good night, Richard.
Richard (*appearing briefly*) Oh, good night, Hugh. See you soon.
Hugh Yes.
Richard (*disappearing*) Now then, you two. That's it. All over.
Sven I think we've missed a splendid bonfire.
Hugh Yes, indeed.
Sven Yes. Yes. You've just moved here, have you?
Hugh That's right.
Sven But you've known Anthea and Richard some time?
Hugh No. We actually only met tonight.
Sven (*nodding*) Uh-huh. Uh-huh.
Hugh Delightful people.
Sven (*neither agreeing or disagreeing*) Yes. Yes. Yes.
Hugh Well, that's certainly my impression.
Sven May I say just one thing? As friends, be careful of them.
Hugh How do you mean?
Sven No. I'll say nothing more. Be careful. Beware. That's all. Good night to you.

Sven goes into the house

Hugh stands for a moment, distinctly puzzled, as—

the CURTAIN *falls*

SCENE 2

The same. Summer, four years later. Sunday morning, very sunny

A game of tennis is in progress. From our restricted viewpoint we see Brian now and then, bobbing about on the base line and receiving service as he and Richard play out the final few points of a "friendly". Richard's voice is heard off from time to time from the other end of the court. Both are dressed for tennis, but casually. Seated on the grass is Mandy, Brian's current girlfriend. At first glance, she is strikingly like Melody. She is younger though and pays very little attention to this world. She is sketching on a sketch block, totally absorbed in her task through most of the scene. Unlike the others, who have made, in their attire, some concession to sunshine, she is draped in shawls, long dresses and a large hat

> *Sven enters, taking the air in his Scandinavian lightweight summer suit and Polaroid sunglasses. He nods approvingly at nature as he walks. A ball clangs into the back fencing of the court*

Brian ... shot ... (*He recovers the ball*)
Richard (*off*) Fluke, I'm afraid. What's that? Thirty-love?
Brian (*flinging back the ball*) Forty-love.
Richard (*off*) Really? Oh.

Sven watches. Brian prepares to receive. Richard serves again. Brian lets it go. A fault. Brian prepares to receive. Richard serves again. Brian runs into the net and returns. We don't see the rest of that rally. It culminates off in a despairing grunt of vain effort from Richard

Richard (*off*) Shot.

Brian returns to our end, looking like a man who has pulled back a point

Sven Good shot. Good shot. Well played, good shot.
Richard (*off*) Forty-fifteen then.

Sven wanders over behind Mandy who ignores him

Sven (*looking at her picture*) Good. Good. Coming along, coming along.

The ball hits the back fencing

Richard (*off*) Damn.

Brian runs in to meet the second service

Sven I would like you to think about this. Art is a lie which makes us realize the truth. Do you know who said that? It was Picasso who said that.
Richard (*off*) Oh, lovely. Forty-thirty.

Brian returns to receive service

Sven I think in some ways you are trying to be too truthful. The result being at the moment that your picture has no truth. Think about that.

Richard's service hits the back fencing

Richard (*off*) Was that in?
Brian Yes.
Richard (*off*) You sure? Looked out from here.
Brian (*gathering up his sweater from the court*) It was in.
Richard (*off*) Play it again if you like.
Brian (*snarling*) It was in.
Sven No, it was in. It was definitely in, Richard, I could see from here. It was in. Not a difficult service to return provided you remember you also have a backhand.

Brian considers killing Sven but resists it

Richard comes into view

Richard You going to have a game this week-end, Sven?
Sven Not this week-end, no. This week-end I want to talk to you, Richard. When is this possible?
Richard Well, I'm going to change and do the lunch now.
Sven This is business, Richard. It's important.
Richard O.K. After lunch then?
Sven Yes but we must leave at four.
Richard O.K. (*He picks up Brian's racket*) Oh no, you weren't playing with this, were you? It's amazing you got a point. Sorry, I meant to throw this away. Mandy, I must ask you. Do you like courgettes?
Mandy Yes, thank you.
Richard Right.

Richard goes

A silence. Sven stands. Brian sits a little apart from Mandy on the grass. Sven wanders and inspects the court from the outside

Sven I think the surface of this court is still not absolutely right. It's too slow. It makes it difficult to play a natural game.

Silence

   Yes.

Sven wanders off past the tennis court

Brian Are you going to be doing that all day?
Mandy Mmm?
Brian What's it meant to be?
Mandy (*imitating Sven*) Truth.
Brian Oh.
Mandy (*still sketching*) Who won?

Brian does not reply

   Is he a good player?
Brian Richard? No. He's rotten. He's the worst player in the world.
Mandy Then why didn't you win?
Brian Because when you're playing Richard, there's no satisfaction in beating him. He's more pleased if you win than if he does. At least if he wins he's apologetic about it. I mean. There's got to be some satisfaction in winning. Otherwise what's the point? He's the only person I know who enjoys genuine loser satisfaction.
Mandy He's very attractive.
Brian Attractive?
Mandy As a personality. Very warm.
Brian Fancy him, do you?
Mandy No, I didn't say that.
Brian Huh.
Mandy That's not what I said. (*Pause*) Anyway, you're a fine one to talk.

Brian How do you mean?
Mandy The way you behave.
Brian What?
Mandy With her.
Brian (*guiltily*) What do you mean?
Mandy You know.
Brian Who?
Mandy Anthea.
Brian Rubbish.
Mandy I don't mind.
Brian I said rubbish.
Mandy It doesn't worry me.
Brian Bloody rubbish.

Anthea and Olive enter, Anthea with the Sunday papers

Anthea Did you win?
Brian (*storming past her*) No.

Brian goes

Anthea I think he lost. Hallo, Mandy. Quite happy?
Mandy Hallo.
Olive Oh, she's drawing. (*Moving behind her*) What's she drawing? What are you drawing, dear?
Mandy I'm just drawing.
Olive Oh, that's nice. She's drawing a lovely picture.
Anthea (*settling in the summerhouse*) Want to read one of these?
Olive No, dear. I never read the papers. I haven't read a paper since I married. I rely on Sven to tell me if there's a war broken out. No, I think there's far too much going on already without reading about it as well. Oh, look at you. I hate you, Anthea, I simply loathe you.
Anthea What?
Olive Look at you. You eat and eat and eat and stay exactly the same. If there was any justice in this world, you would be like a barrel.
Anthea I'm just lucky, that's all.
Olive Yes. I can't eat anything. Nothing. Not a thing. It's not fair. It really isn't. I could kill you.

A pause. Anthea reads. Mandy draws. Olive fidgets

Lovely day for drawing, isn't it? I say, it's a lovely day for drawing.
Mandy Mmm.
Olive Oh, I wish I could draw. I've always wanted to draw. I'd've given my right arm to be able to draw. It must be very relaxing.
Anthea Why don't you have a go?
Olive Oh, no, no, no. Too late now. I leave things like that to Sven. Sven can draw quite well, you know. He might have been an artist at one time. Only there's not a lot of future in it. Oh, look at that girl. Look at her. Look at that figure. I could kill her.

Sven appears

Sven Ahhh ...

Olive Ahhh ...

Sven Now, now, Olive. You mustn't disturb our little artist.

Olive Oh, there you are.

Sven Very pleasant. Very pleasant indeed.

Anthea We'll have drinks when the Emersons arrive. Unless you fancy one now.

Sven No, no. Too early. Yes, I presume Hugh Emerson will be somewhere in the middle of his sermon by now.

Anthea Yes, I suppose so.

Sven Well. For me one visit was enough. I'm certainly glad we're not there today.

Olive Oh dear, yes.

Anthea Well, he does try his best.

Sven No, no, Anthea. It was the most appalling rubbish. The man was not only inarticulate but he was often totally inaccurate. He managed to bore you, mystify you and misinform you all in one breath.

Anthea Yes, but he does sort of mean it, doesn't he? I mean, he's very sincere.

Sven A couple of hundred years ago they would simply have burnt him for heresy.

Anthea He is a bit of a woffler, I must say. He's not going down awfully well, poor love.

Olive No. We noticed when we were there.

Anthea I think he's a bit radical for this village. I mean, all the congregation are four times his age. They see him as a sort of teenage tearaway. Richard and I give him all the support we can but I think we're fighting a losing battle.

Sven Now, Anthea. Has Richard mentioned our present problems to you?

Anthea What about? The business?

Sven Yes, indeed.

Anthea Oh. He didn't say there were any problems.

Sven Well, I'm afraid there are.

Anthea Oh dear. Serious?

Sven They could become so if we don't discuss them together. Now, it is a fact there are four directors of The Scandinavian Craftware Co. Ltd. Richard, myself, you and Olive. Though naturally you and Olive are not strictly active partners. Nonetheless, in the case of Richard and myself, we are equal partners and it is vital that we discuss everything together. Not, as Richard has been doing, acting on his own individual whims. Making unilateral decisions which could quite easily have bankrupted the firm.

Anthea Has he done that?

Sven Thank heavens, no. More through luck than good judgement, he has actually lost us very little. In fact, to be strictly accurate, he has made us a little. In fact, he has made us quite a nice little sum and he has incidentally found us a new outlet for Swedish glassware. Nevertheless, these decisions were irrational, made without reference to known trading conditions, the present state of the world market or, more important, to me.

Olive Sven's very worried.

Anthea I should talk to Richard.

Sven I have been trying to talk to Richard. If I can get his attention for five minutes, I will talk to him with pleasure.

Olive Sven's quite serious about this, Anthea. He's quite serious.

Anthea Yes, yes.

Olive I mean, Sven wouldn't say this unless he was very worried. I know Sven.

Sven Not unless I was very, very, very worried I wouldn't say this.

Anthea Well, I'm sure Richard will see your point of view. He's never difficult.

Sven Anthea, I'm not saying he is difficult. I have endless respect for Richard. Endless respect. But he must be made to understand that I cannot remain in partnership with a man who doesn't totally trust me.

Brian enters with two croquet mallets

Brian (*to Anthea*) Excuse me. The kids say you promised them a game of croquet before lunch.

Anthea Did I? Oh lord, yes, I think I did.

Olive Now, don't you go jumping up, Anthea. You spoil them.

Anthea No, I promised.

Brian It's you and Debbie against Giles and me. Penny a hoop.

Anthea Oh no.

Brian And they're also saying that if Christopher Emerson is coming to lunch, they're going to hide all their toys.

Anthea Oh dear. They don't like Christopher at all. He's quite nice now.

Brian He's awful.

Anthea Well, fairly awful. (*Going*) All right, all right, I bags be blue.

Brian and Anthea go

Olive Debbie's growing up, isn't she?

Sven Mmm.

Olive She's, what, nearly ten. Well, they're adults by that age these days, aren't they? Are you going to play tennis today?

Sven Not today, my darling, no.

Olive Every time we come down here, I pack all your stuff. Your rackets and your gym shoes. You never use them.

Sven Not today, my darling. There are other problems.

Olive She shouldn't spoil those children like she does though. Everything they ask for, they get. It isn't right. They'll grow up with a false sense of values.

Sven No. Nobody should have everything they want. Not even you, my darling. (*He kisses her*)

Louise comes from the direction of the tennis court. She is in her church clothes but is somewhat flustered

Louise I know we're late. It can't be helped.

Olive Late?

Louise Hallo, Olive. Hallo, Sven.

Sven Dear Louise, hallo.

Louise It can't be helped. He's just being absolutely impossible. The little brute, he just screamed and yelled. I had to leave him to Hugh. He's getting too strong for me now. He's eight years old and when he punches you, it really hurts.

Olive Is this Christopher?

Louise Yes. So anyway, I'm afraid we're late. And Hugh will be even later.

Olive You're not late.

Louise Oh. I thought we were supposed to be ...

Sven After four years of living next door to these people, you still expect their meals to be on time? Time is nothing in this house.

Louise Oh well.

Olive Sit down, Louise. Get your breath. That's a lovely outfit.

Louise Oh, do you think so? I-um-I've got a great bruise here. (*Pulling up her sleeve*) Look ... (*She sees Mandy*) Oh ...

Olive Oh, you wouldn't have met Mandy. This is Brian's new friend, Mandy. She's down for the week-end.

Mandy Hallo.

Louise How do you do?

Olive This is Mrs Emerson, Mandy. Louise.

Louise What's she doing?

Olive She's drawing a picture. It's very good. (*In an undertone*) She's an art student but quite pleasant.

Louise Oh.

Olive And how was your service?

Louise My what?

Olive Isn't that what you've been doing? Your Morning Service?

Louise Oh yes. Oh, very good. Disappointing turn-out but I think it's the time of the year too. A lot of people are on holiday.

Sven Hum—hum—hum ...

Olive Your husband preached the sermon, did he?

Louise Yes, yes.

Olive A good one, was it?

Louise Er—yes—yes, not—quite—very good, yes. He—er—well, to be honest, he's getting better of course, but I don't think his sermon's his strongest point. He admits that. He goes over them with me in bed—I mean, you know, when we're alone—and they're quite marvellous. You know he's speaking just for you and you can see his eyes and that he really means everything he says and it's awfully important ... but directly he gets up there, in front of all those people, he seems to get all tense. You know, and you can't see his eyes because he tends to keep them closed and then he speaks so fast, it's difficult to hear what he's saying sometimes. Particularly for a lot of the people there because they're quite elderly. And someone shouted at him to speak up the other day and that really did upset him because he does try awfully hard. Really.

Olive We found him very good indeed.

Louise Did you? Oh, that's nice. That is nice to hear. I'll tell him that. People don't say a lot, you know, except to criticize. And you wonder ... I had to leave him to deal with Christopher. He's going to get Mrs Gregson to sit in.

Olive We would have come to church only we overslept, I'm afraid.

Louise Oh. That's all right.

Olive Our one day off.

Louise Yes.

A scream from Anthea off. A blue croquet ball rolls on

Anthea (*off*) Oh, you brute, Giles, you little brute.

Anthea enters with a croquet mallet

Oh no, look. I'm right down here. Oh, hallo, Louise. You've arrived. Splendid.

Louise Hallo.

Anthea Before you go, remind me to give you those envelopes. I've done them all.

Louise Oh, wonderful. You needn't have ...

Anthea Is Hugh with you?

Louise He's coming. He's just seeing to Christopher.

Anthea Isn't Christopher coming?

Louise No. He's not feeling on top form. Hugh's getting Mrs Gregson to sit with him.

Anthea Oh dear. Sad. (*Shouting*) Debbie! Debbie darling, will you ask Daddy to give you the drinks to bring out ... Quickly, darling. No, we'll wait for you. We won't play without you. Promise. (*To the others*) We're playing this absurd game of croquet. Every time I get near a hoop, Giles bashes me to kingdom come. Look at me. I can't even see the lawn. Anyone else want a swing?

Sven No, no. I think to win this game, you need inside knowledge of the local conditions.

Anthea When are we going to see you on the tennis court, Sven?

Sven I think not today.

Anthea Oh, come on. I don't believe all this talk about you being a great player.

Sven Now, be fair, Anthea, be fair. You never heard me say I was a great player.

Anthea We've been hearing it for years. Every time you come down.

Sven If I may correct you, what I said was that I was a good player. Not a great player.

Olive He was a champion.

Sven No, my darling. I must correct you too. I was a junior champion.

Olive Junior champion.

Sven For three years running.

Louise This was for all of Sweden, was it?

Sven No. It was not for all of Sweden. I come from Finland.

Louise You were champion of all Finland?

Sven Well. Nearly all Finland. There were some parts of Finland that didn't compete. Let us say, most of Finland.

Anthea Well, I'll believe it when I see it.

Sven One day. One day. You wait ...

Richard enters, now dressed for cooking, carrying a tray with a jug of fruit cup and some glasses

Richard Morning, all. Mind your backs. (*He puts the tray on the table*)

Anthea Why didn't you get Debbie to carry them?

Richard Because she nearly dropped them. Can you help yourselves everyone? I'm in the midst. Lunch in ten minutes. Louise, do you like courgettes?

Louise Yes, I think so.

Richard Good. You've got them. Right. (*He moves back towards the house and shifts the croquet ball to a better position*) I'll have you know Giles has been cheating. I saw him. I'd cheat as well if I were you.

Richard sprints off

Olive Well—er—shall I pour? I don't know what it is.

Anthea It looks like his fruit cup.

Olive (*pouring*) Oh. It smells nice. Louise?

Louise Thank you. A little.

Anthea (*looking over Mandy's shoulder*) I like that.

Mandy Thank you.

Olive Anthea? (*She proffers a glass*)

Anthea Please. (*She takes one*)

Olive Some for—um—Mandy?

Mandy What?

Olive Do you want some of this?

Mandy No, thanks.

Anthea She's immensely sensible, this girl. She doesn't drink.

Olive Oh, how wise.

Louise Very sensible.

Brian enters with his croquet mallet

Brian Anthea, it's your go.

Anthea Oh, all right. (*Handing Brian her glass*) Hold that, will you?

Brian We're going to have to stop in a minute. He wants the kids in to help serve up.

Anthea Right. (*Calling*) All right, Giles, I'm coming to get you. (*She hits the ball. To Brian*) We'll stop after the next hoop.

Anthea goes out

Olive Would you like a glass, Brian?

Brian I'll be back in a second. Thanks.

Brian goes off

Louise Is Brian still working for you?

Sven Yes, yes. He's working for Richard and me. In the office. He's very good. Quite bright. Not very forthcoming but he does a good job.

Louise I find him a funny person, really. He never seems to want ... (*She looks over at Mandy*) Yes, anyway ...

Sven Yes, well, enough said. Cheers.

They drink

Olive Oh, it's really very pleasant.
Louise Oh, yes it is. It's very nice, yes.
Olive Refreshing.
Louise Yes.
Olive What do you think, Sven?
Sven (*tasting it carefully*) Yes. Yes. It's pleasant. A little bit...
Olive Yes. Yes. (*She sits at the table*)
Sven Bland. A little bland, perhaps.
Olive Yes, I suppose it's a little bit bland.
Louise Yes, I know what you mean. (*She sits at the table*)
Sven It is in danger of becoming watery.
Louise Watery.
Sven In my opinion. (*He sits next to Louise*)
Olive Yes, it is a bit watery. I could have done with a bit more taste.
Louise Yes, I wouldn't want too much of it.
Olive No.
Sven No.
Louise No.

A pause

Olive I hope your husband's not going to miss his lunch.
Louise Oh, he'll be along.
Olive Mind you, from what I know of him, I can't see him missing a square
meal. He's certainly got an appetite.
Louise Yes.
Olive I like a man to have an appetite.
Louise Yes, he certainly has when he comes here.
Olive Oh. Doesn't he at home? Eat, I mean?
Louise No, not overmuch.
Olive Well, that's disappointing for you. I mean, if you go to all that trouble.
Louise Yes, it is sometimes.
Olive Mind you, this one's a devil. Over his food. Aren't you? You're a devil.
Sven No, darling, not a devil. I just like first rate food, beautifully cooked.
Like you cook it, most of the time.
Olive Oh, get on.
Sven She's jealous because I'm a better cook than she is. I can't help that.
That's the way it is.
Olive Oh yes, he's a wonderful cook.
Louise Is he?
Olive Oh wonderful. With Finnish things, of course.
Sven Well, of course with Finnish things. I'm Finnish. I'm not going to cook
steak and kidney Yorkshire puddings or whatever.
Olive (*laughing*) Steak and kidney Yorkshire puddings. Get on.
Louise (*rising and moving to behind Mandy*) I'm sorry, I can't resist it. I must
just peep and see what she's... (*She studies Mandy's picture*) Oh yes, that's

very ... very good indeed. Yes, that is nice. What's this down here, dear? Down here? This?

Mandy That's grass there.

Louise Grass. Oh yes. No, I meant this thing here. This thing.

Mandy That's a snake.

Louise A snake?

Mandy Yes.

Louise A grass snake?

Mandy No, just a snake in the grass.

Louise Oh. Unusual. (*She withdraws*) She's drawing snakes.

Olive Snakes, ugh.

Sven Well, perhaps the girl sees snakes. Who knows?

Olive Good job she hasn't drunk this stuff.

Louise (*laughing*) Yes ...

Hugh enters from behind the tennis court. He has his hand bandaged with a handkerchief

Hugh Hallo. Sorry, everyone. You're all waiting for me, no doubt. I'm sorry.

Louise Hugh ...

Olive No, no. You're just right. Just in time.

Hugh Oh splendid.

Olive (*pouring*) Will you have a glass of this?

Hugh Er—oh, is it er ...?

Sven I should think the alcoholic content is non-existent.

Hugh Oh well, fair enough. I don't want to be hung over for Evensong.

Louise (*sotto voce*) How is he?

Hugh He's all right. Mrs Gregson's with him.

Louise What happened to your hand?

Hugh Oh, he was being—very difficult, very stubborn ...

Louise Are you all right? (*She sits*)

Hugh He bit me. It's not serious. He didn't know what he was doing. He just bit without thinking. (*Taking the glass proffered by Olive*) Thank you very much. Good health.

Anthea enters with her glass

Anthea I think this is absolutely delicious and I am going to have some more. Hugh, you're here. (*She kisses him on the cheek*) I love Hugh on Sundays. He's all pink and shiny.

Hugh (*embarrassed*) I don't think I'm any more ...

Louise Do you want to sit down, Anthea?

Anthea No, I've only come for a refill. Then I'm going to help. (*Refilling her glass*) Now, has everyone been asked if they like courgettes? Hugh?

Hugh Oh yes, rather.

Anthea Because you can have sprouts.

Hugh No. Courgettes are fine.

Louise They wouldn't be fine if I offered them to you.

Hugh You've never offered them to me.

Louise No, because I know what you'd say if I did.

Hugh Yes, well ...

Brian enters

Anthea (*on her way again*) Help yourself, Brian.
Brian Right.
Anthea We'll give you a yell, folks.

Anthea goes

Olive (*proffering a glass*) Brian.
Brian Thank you (*He sits on the grass by Mandy*)

Pause

Olive Well, I must say, I do enjoy my week-ends down here. We always enjoy
   them, don't we, Sven?
Sven Yes, yes.
Brian Very peaceful.
Louise Yes, it's a lovely spot.
Hugh Yes.

Pause

Olive It's a pity your little Christopher couldn't come to lunch.
Hugh Yes, he's ...
Louise I was saying, he's a little under the weather.
Hugh Yes.
Olive Poor little mite. How old is he now?
Louise Eight. Eight-and-a-half.
Olive Oh. Young Debbie's shot up, hasn't she?
Louise Oh yes.
Olive Quite the young lady now. Little Giles is growing.
Hugh Yes.
Brian Yes.
Louise They're very lucky.
Olive Oh yes.
Louise I mean, there's no reason why they should necessarily have turned out
   such nice children.
Olive There's no law, no.
Hugh Well, I suppose they're very pleasant parents, so ....
Louise That doesn't always follow.
Hugh Well ...
Sven No, no, she's right. It doesn't always follow. But there it is. Richard
   and Anthea are some of the lucky ones. They accept it without question.
   If you like, they take it for granted.
Olive Yes, they do rather, don't they?
Louise What?
Olive Take things for granted a little bit. I mean, they've been very lucky.
Louise Well, yes. Good luck to them.
Olive Oh quite. But, well, with the children—I mean, they take very little

trouble with them as far as I can see. They let them do very much what they want.

Louise Yes, they do. They do. I mean, we could never let Christopher run wild.

Olive Oh, and I could kill her for that figure of hers.

Sven Now, the woman can't help her figure, darling.

Olive She eats like a horse, too.

Louise Well, I think they eat too much, frankly. I mean, as soon as you arrive here it's food, drink, food, drink.

Hugh Oh, I don't know.

Olive Well, as you say, good luck to them.

Louise Yes, good luck to them.

Sven I think I must disagree. I think I would go a little further than luck, you know. It's not just luck.

Olive Oh no. They know what they want.

Louise Oh yes.

Olive Richard's got his head screwed on.

Sven Oh yes. Don't be fooled by Richard. He's nobody's fool. He works quietly at it and gets what he wants.

Brian True.

Sven You agree with me?

Brian Oh yes, he usually gets what he wants.

Olive Well, so does she.

Louise Yes, well, she's certainly taken us over. I mean, it started with just a helping hand but now they're running everything.

Hugh Oh no, I don't know that ...

Louise The first day we were here, they burnt our fence down.

Hugh Well, yes ...

Louise Let's face it, what are we doing here now, Hugh? I mean, I don't mind being here but would we be here but for them? No, we would be getting on with our own lives like we should be. I mean, we spend more time here than we do in our own home.

Hugh Well, yes, but ...

Sven Remember the first time we met? Remember I said to you, beware.

Hugh Yes, yes.

Sven They are nice people but they are invidious people. They have to take people over. And why? Because eventually they want to own people.

Olive Yes, that is true. That is very true.

Brian Yes, yes.

Sven And they do it in this very pleasant way. In this friendly way. But the motive itself is that most selfish of human motives, the desire for power over other people. I know this. I am in business with him.

Olive And that business would collapse without Sven.

Brian I'd say that was certainly true of Richard.

Louise Well, I'm sorry. I know this is a dreadful thing to say but I have never trusted her one inch.

Hugh Well ...

Louise I'm sorry, Hugh. Not one inch.

Olive I'm afraid as far as I'm concerned that goes for both of them. I mean, I love them dearly but ...
Sven I think your instincts, unfortunately, are probably right.
Brian Probably, yes.
Hugh Well—yes. Well ...

A slight pause

Anthea enters

Anthea Grub up, everyone.
Olive Oh goody, I'm starving.

There is a general rise and stirring, except for Mandy

Anthea Sorry we're late. You can't hurry the chef when he's being creative. Could you bring your glasses with you in case you want wine. We're sparing the washers-up.

Richard appears behind Anthea

Richard Could they bring their glasses?
Anthea I've just asked them, darling.
Richard Oh, splendid.
Sven Wait, wait, wait. A drink for the chef.
Olive (*pouring*) Oh yes. For the chef.
Richard Well, thank you. But if I don't get back to the kitchen, it'll be ... (*Taking the glass*) Thank you. God bless. *Bon appetit.* (*He takes a hasty swill*) It'll be stone cold. Follow me.

Richard goes out. Olive and Louise follow

Olive Nothing but eat, drink and be merry. Isn't it wonderful?
Anthea Coming, Hugh?
Hugh Yes, yes ...
Anthea Cheer up. We love you.
Hugh Yes. Right.

Hugh goes

Anthea Sven?
Sven You go on, my darling. I'm going to be supremely helpful and bring the tray.
Anthea Sven, you're tremendous.

Anthea goes

Brian (*to Mandy*) Are you coming?
Mandy In a minute.
Brian Okay. Suit yourself.

Brian goes out

Sven picks up the tray, moves towards the house and stops to look over Mandy's shoulder

Sven (*studying her picture*) Yes, yes. That is an improvement. That is a great improvement. That is now a good picture. You see? You can do it. Good. Clever girl.

Sven goes out

Mandy finishes with her drawing, holds it at arm's length to study it, closes one eye, then the other. Scowls and, without ceremony, tears the picture into pieces and goes in for lunch, as—

the CURTAIN *falls*

ACT II

SCENE 1

The same. Boxing Day, four years later. A rainy, grey afternoon. Activity on the tennis court. An eccentric, rather drunken game is in progress: at this end, Anthea, in plastic rain hat, tennis gear and gumboots partnering Richard, dressed in more conventional tennis kit except for a long scarf wrapped round several times and gloves; at the other end, Brian and Mo, his latest girl-friend, at present both out of sight. A lot of shrieks and yells. A ball hits the back fencing. Anthea vainly tries to intercept it

Mo (*off*) Yahoo!
Anthea Aaaah! It's these boots. I can't run in these boots.
Richard Fancy playing in boots.
Anthea I'm not playing in shoes, it's soaking wet. Soaking.
Brian (*off*) Our service.
Richard You're not still scoring?
Brian (*off*) Five three. Second set.
Mo (*off*) To us.
Richard This ball's so wet, it won't even bounce.
Anthea It's stopped raining.
Richard You wouldn't know it.
Brian (*off*) Ready?
Richard Ready. What a ridiculous way to spend Christmas.
Brian (*off*) Right.
Richard Anthea, yours.

The ball again hits the back fencing

Anthea (*chasing, breathless*) Oh, I'm too old. I'm too old.
Mo (*off*) Old? Who's old?
Richard She's very, very old. (*Mock sotto voce*) Thirty-four.
Mo (*off, loudly*) Thirty-four?
Richard (*even more loudly*) Thirty-four.
Anthea (*attacking Richard with her racket*) Shut up, shut up, shut up.
Brian (*off*) Right ... Whoops.
Anthea Where did that go?
Mo (*off*) Oh, well served. Well served, partner.
Brian (*off*) Somebody in this court is drunk and it's not me.
Richard Second service. (*To Anthea*) It's no use standing back there, dear. He can hardly get the ball over the net as it is.
Brian (*off*) Coming up.
Anthea (*rushing in to meet the serve, whirling her racket*) Wheee!

The game continues. Anthea and Richard bound into view occasionally but most of it is sounds off, the ball rarely reaching the back of the court

Sven enters from the house, unsteadily. He is supported by Olive. At thirty-eight and thirty-six respectively, they have both put on a bit of weight. Sven is looking rather green. Olive still wears her paper hat

Olive Breathe in. Get some air in you. Take deep breaths.

Sven I'm fine, my darling. I am perfectly all right. You don't have to propel me round the garden.

Anthea (*coming into view and gathering up a ball at the back of the court*) Hallo. Have you revived?

Olive Yes.

Anthea You were both fast asleep on the sofa. We left you.

Sven A little too much of your plum pudding.

Olive Too much booze ...

Sven No, darling. I had very little booze indeed. Very little.

Anthea Have a walk round. It's cleared up, anyway. We'll have some tea and Christmas cake in a minute. (*She disappears*)

Sven Oh, my God. That woman never stops producing food. She's obsessed with food.

Olive And look at her. Just look at her. Like a stick. When I think I spend fifty-one weeks of the year on a diet—oh, I could throttle her.

Anthea comes into view, chasing a ball

Anthea Hallo!

Olive Hallo.

Anthea moves out of sight

Feeling better?

Sven Fine, my darling. I am feeling perfectly rosy.

Olive You don't look it. You've been very peaky lately. Can't we have a proper holiday sometime?

Sven Well, there's nothing to stop us certainly.

Olive Do us both good.

Sven The way the firm is going, I could probably take a year off, no one would notice the difference.

Olive Hardly.

Sven It's perfectly true, my darling. Over the past few years, I have been reduced to nothing more than a piece of glorified office furniture.

Olive Oh, I'm not listening to this.

Sven It's absolutely true.

Olive Rubbish.

Sven This firm now runs completely without my help. Let's face it. Let us face it.

Olive Ssh. Ssh.

Richard (*appearing momentarily to pick up a ball*) Hallo.

Sven Hallo.

Olive Hallo.

Richard disappears

Sven That man there, my excellent partner, runs the whole business in his sleep. He's never in the office. He neglects to turn up for important meetings. He fails to read anything that's sent to him. And even if he does, he doesn't reply. And yet, yet, he thinks he knows more about the whole thing than we do who are there in the office working seven days a week. And the ironical thing, my darling, is that he does. Every damn decision he makes is invariably right. People like Brian there, me, we are the pen-pushers. Totally dispensable, believe me.

Olive (*rather tearfully*) I wish you wouldn't go on like this. You know I don't like it when you go on like this.

Sven I'm sorry, my darling, I'm sorry.

Olive It's not like you to run yourself down.

Sven But I am always objective. I am first and foremost objective.

Olive I'm going in.

Sven Yes, go in, go in. Please go in. And take off that ridiculous hat.

Olive (*taking it off*) Oh, I forgot I had it on. I must ... I wish you wouldn't, Sven.

Olive goes in

Brian (*off*) Game.

Richard (*coming into view*) Well played, well played.

Anthea (*also coming into sight*) Is it over?

Richard It's over!

Anthea Thank God! (*She pauses to put on her mac, which is hanging up in the tennis court*)

Mo bounds into view. She has rolled-up jeans, unsuitable shoes, striped socks, a tee shirt and a combat hat

Mo We won, we won, we won.

Sven What are you ridiculous lot playing at?

Anthea Underwater tennis. It's very difficult.

Sven Your children are the only sane people in this house. Sitting in the dry in front of the fire, watching the television.

Brian comes into view

Brian You going to have a game, Sven?

Richard I don't think Sven looks in form this afternoon.

Sven No, no. Don't you be too sure, Richard. Don't be too sure.

Richard Sorry. I thought you looked a bit ...

Sven I'm rosy, I'm rosy.

Richard Good. Good.

Sven In fact, maybe I will have a game, yes.

Richard Are you sure? It'll be dark in a minute.

Sven No, no. I'll have you a game, Richard. We'll see. Who knows? Maybe in tennis I can still teach you something, eh?

Richard (*without trace of acrimony*) Okay.

Anthea Ah-ha. Lessons from the Finnish Junior Champion, Richard.

Sven Now, now, now. You can laugh, Anthea my darling, you can laugh.

Anthea No, Sven, I ...
Sven We shall see. Maybe the laughter will stop.
Richard Sven, she didn't mean ...
Sven We shall see, Mrs Clever, we shall see. Now, I shall change. Wait for me.

  Sven goes

Brian What was that about?
Anthea Darling, do you think he ought to play?
Richard Why not?
Anthea Well, he's had a bit to drink.
Richard So have I.
Anthea Yes, but for Sven... You know he gets fighting drunk on Vichy water.
Mo (*approaching*) What was the matter with him?
Anthea We were just wondering whether Sven ought to play. Actually, Olive hinted that he has been drinking lately. I mean, she didn't say that because Olive would never say a word against Sven but she sort of hinted.
Richard Oh. I hadn't noticed.
Mo What are we doing now?
Richard Well—er—I think I'm about to play another game of tennis.
Mo I'll play you then.
Richard No, I'm playing Sven.
Mo No, you're not. You're playing with me. Come on, you play with me. (*She clutches on to Richard*)
Richard Hang on.
Anthea (*amused*) Mo, don't. He's playing with Sven.
Mo You mind your own business, you. He's playing with me, aren't you?
Richard No, I'm ...
Brian (*embarrassed*) Mo, come on. (*He takes hold of her*)
Mo Oh, get off.
Brian Come on, Mo.
Mo Get off.
Anthea (*also grabbing Mo*) Come on, Mo. Let go.
Mo I'm playing with him.
Richard (*disentangling himself*) I'll change into some dry things.

  Richard flees towards the house

Anthea (*still rather amused*) Yes, do, darling. Come on, Mo—Mo...
Mo Let go. You let go.
Brian Mo! Mo! Look leave her to me, Anthea, will you? Leave her to me.
Anthea Pleasure. Let her sit for a minute till she's calmed down.
Mo Yes, you bugger off, you.
Anthea Certainly, yes. Fine, good-bye. (*As she goes*) My God.

  Anthea goes off after Richard

Brian (*still clutching Mo*) Are you going to sit still?
Mo Yes.
Brian Promise.

Mo Yes.
Brian Promise then.
Mo I promise.
Brian (*releasing her*) All right. Sit still.

Mo sits on the summer house steps

Mo Oh, I feel ill. It's all that food.
Brian What do you expect? You ate like a pig. (*He sits beside her*)
Mo I am a pig.
Brian What did you behave like that for?
Mo When?
Brian Just now.
Mo Felt like it.
Brian Why?
Mo You wouldn't understand if I told you.
Brian Why not?
Mo You're too old.
Brian Too old?
Mo You're over thirty.
Brian What's that got to do with it?
Mo If you're over thirty, then you're too old. You've forgotten what it's like.
Brian What what's like?
Mo To be under thirty.
Brian Oh, great.
Mo Oh, I feel terrible.
Brian Serve you right.
Mo You known these people long?
Brian Yes. I've known Anthea for—ten years ...
Mo Oh.
Brian I knew her before she met Richard. I met her when she was married before. She's not married to Richard, you see.
Mo (*not very interested*) Oh.
Brian She was married before and then—she broke up with him. She was very unhappy then. And she had the two kids and nowhere much to go. I had a couple of rooms at that time in Gloucester Road and she rang me, she must have been desperate, because I'd met her briefly through her husband—Matthew. And she said, did I know of anywhere. And I said, well, there's here. I mean, you can muck in here for a few weeks—no obligations. And so she came. It was mad, really mad. I mean, four of us in two rooms and the kids wouldn't sleep and we both sat up and talked all night and—she was magic. Just a magic lady. And we went on like that for weeks. I used to drive a mini-cab in those days. And I'd come home and there she'd be with Debbie and Giles and it was the happiest time I've ever had in my life. Then Richard came and that was that. I never told her, you see. What I felt. Because I'd promised at the beginning there'd be no obligation. So I said nothing to her at all. Not until it was too late. I think I sort of hoped she'd guess what I felt but she couldn't have done and she went with Richard and that was that.

A silence

Mo Oh, I've got a pain in me guts.
Brian (*rising*) Okay, come on. I'll get you in. I'll get you indoors. (*He helps her up*)
Mo Ooooh.

Brian steers Mo towards the house.

They pass Anthea coming out

Anthea Better?
Brian She'll be all right. Come on.
Mo I'm coming.
Anthea Richard's left his jacket.

Brian and Mo go out

Anthea goes into the tennis court and collects Richard's jacket

Hugh and Louise enter from the side of the tennis court, off on their Boxing Day walk

Anthea Hallo ... !
Hugh 'Scuse us. Just cutting through.
Anthea Off on a walk?
Louise Just a quick one.
Anthea Have a nice Christmas?
Hugh Yes, yes. Not too bad. We have Louise's mother with us so we've been quite busy.
Anthea How is she?
Louise Oh, very well. We left her playing chess with Christopher.
Anthea Does he play chess? How impressive. Ours can only just manage four letter scrabble.
Hugh Oh, Christopher's really very good. Too good for me, now, I'm afraid. I think he's got a talent quite definitely.
Anthea Marvellous.
Louise It takes a certain sort of mind.
Anthea Yes. Not mine, I'm afraid.
Hugh Did we hear you playing tennis earlier?
Anthea Oh yes, sorry. Were we very rowdy?
Hugh No, no. It just seemed very energetic for Boxing Day.
Louise (*anxious to move on*) Yes, well, we must ...
Hugh Yes.
Anthea Mind you, if you stick around, you might witness a classic encounter.
Hugh What's that?
Anthea Sven is about to make his debut on the tennis court.
Hugh Really?
Anthea At long last. Sven v. Richard.
Louise It's a bit wet for tennis, isn't it?
Anthea Not for Finnish tennis.
Hugh I say, perhaps we ought to stay and see them.

Louise I thought we were going for a walk.
Hugh We will.
Louise It'll be dark soon.
Anthea Well, don't ruin your day. It's not that important.

Olive comes from the house, agitated

Olive Anthea, I don't know what's got in to you and Richard, I really don't.
Anthea Sorry?
Olive Encouraging Sven to play tennis.
Anthea Me?
Olive He's in no condition. He's in no fit state.
Anthea I haven't said a thing.
Olive He'd never have agreed to it without encouragement.
Anthea Well, I don't see how I ...
Olive He hasn't taken any exercise for ten years. What'll this do to him?
Anthea Well, I'll try and stop it then if you like.
Olive You'd better. It'll kill him.
Hugh Perhaps he ought to be a little careful.
Olive Of course he should. He's thirty-eight, you know. Thirty-eight. That's the age they have to watch it.
Hugh Oh really?

Sven enters in a borrowed tennis gear, made for a man a trifle slimmer

Sven All right, all right. Where's the opposition?
Hugh Oh, bravo!
Anthea Oh gosh. Is that the best we could find for you?
Sven These are perfectly adequate, Anthea. Provided I do no sudden arm movements.
Olive Oh, Sven.
Sven Where is he, then? I'm ready for him.
Olive Please, Sven, do be careful.
Sven What's the woman talking about. I'm going to play a game of tennis, my darling, that's all. You would think I was going out for a gunfight.
Anthea I don't think you should play for too long, Sven. If it's your first for some time.
Sven It won't be for too long. Don't worry. A few love games, it'll all be over. Good afternoon, Louise. Good afternoon, Hugh.
Hugh Hallo.
Louise Hallo.
Hugh You look—ready for action ...
Sven I'm ready, yes. (*He goes into the court and starts a few knee bends*) Hup, hup, hup, hup ...
Olive He shouldn't be playing. He really shouldn't.
Louise Are you coming ?
Hugh I thought we might watch.
Louise No, I want to go for a walk.
Hugh In a moment.
Louise I want to deliver these envelopes round the Crescent anyway.

Anthea Oh, you can leave those here if you like. I'll do them when I do the others.
Louise No, I'll do them.
Anthea Well, I'm delivering the others first thing tomorrow, I'll ...
Louise I'll do them. I'm not totally incapable, you know, Anthea.
Anthea No, of course not.
Hugh She was only offering, dear.
Sven Hup, hup, hup, hup, hup ...
Olive The first time I haven't packed his tennis gear and he decides to play.

Brian is dragged from the house by Mo

Mo Come on, then. Come on.
Brian All right, all right. I'm coming.
Anthea She's recovered.
Brian (*sourly*) She's recovered.
Sven Ah, Brian. Good. Just the man we need. An umpire, please.
Brian Oh come on, Sven.
Sven No, seriously. We need an umpire. This game must be played properly. Fair play must be seen to be done.
Brian You don't need me.
Mo Go on.
Sven Come on. Come, come, come.
Brian All right, all right.

Brian goes into the court. Mo loiters outside

Anthea Are the kids coming out?
Mo No. They're watching some boring old love film in black and white.

Brian and Mo exit

Anthea Oh well.
Sven Come on. Where's the opposition? I'm getting chilly out here.
Anthea He had to change, Sven. He was soaked through from the last game.
Sven Well, I can't wait all day.
Anthea He's taking this awfully seriously.
Olive That's the trouble. I think he is serious.
Louise Well, I'm going to walk on up and deliver these.
Hugh Oh, all right then.
Louise No, you stay and watch if you want. I'll be all right on my own. I'll see you back home.
Hugh I could follow on and meet you.
Louise If you want to. Good-bye.
Anthea You off, Louise?
Louise I'd better deliver these before it gets dark. It's not well lit in the Crescent.
Sven Louise, you're not staying to see the great victory?
Louise No. Sorry, I can't. Some of us just don't have time for playing games. Much as we might like to.

Louise goes out. Mo enters

Mo (*chanting*) Why are we waiting? Why are we waiting? Why are we waiting?

Mo disappears

Olive Oh, that little girl's terribly rowdy, isn't she? I don't know where Brian finds them.
Anthea Well, he likes variety, I think.
Olive I don't know about variety. They all look alike to me.

Richard enters in fresh tennis kit

Richard Sorry.
Sven Ah-ha! At last!
Mo Hooray.
Richard Sorry, couldn't find my old shoes.
Sven Come along, come along.
Richard All right.
Anthea Richard ...
Richard Mmm?
Anthea Make it a short game, please. Sven's very out of condition.
Richard All right, don't worry.
Sven Come on, come on.

Brian appears

Richard Make it the best of five games, shall we?
Sven Best of five? What are you talking about? This is a major tournament.
Olive No, Sven, make it the best of five.
Sven No such thing.
Brian Best of five. Umpire's decision.
Sven How can we ...
Brian Umpire's decision.
Richard Umpire's decision.
Mo (*chanting*) Off—off—off—off ...
Brian Shut up.
Olive (*shadowing Sven outside the court fencing, anxiously*) Now take it gently, dear, take it gently.
Sven I have no intention of taking anything gently, my darling.
Brian (*producing a coin*) Spin for service. Call.
Richard Heads.
Brian Heads it is.
Sven I'll take this end.

Brian exits inside the court, presumably to stand square with the net

Richard Change after three?
Sven Fine with me.
Olive Sven ...
Richard Want a knock-up?
Sven Just one or two.

Richard (*going off to the other end*) I warn you, the ball hardly bounces at all, so watch it.

Richard exits to the other end of the court

Sven Right.

Mo moves off outside after Richard

Brian (*off*) Play.
Richard (*off*) Ready?
Sven Right. (*He runs in and back. Off*) My God.
Richard (*off*) I warned you.
Sven (*returning*) It's like playing with a cannon ball.
Anthea I know, it's quite impossible.
Olive Be careful, Sven.
Sven My darling, will you please, please, please be quiet. (*He runs in to return a shot*)

Olive moves after him

Richard (*off*) Sorry. Shot.
Mo (*off*) Come on, Richard. We want Richard.
Anthea We're all worrying about Sven. This is the second game Richard's played today.
Hugh He's pretty fit, isn't he?
Anthea Well, fairly.
Sven (*off*) All right, let's start. Can we start, please?
Richard Fine.
Brian Okay.
Hugh I—er—was hoping to catch you actually. Anthea—I ...
Anthea Oh, they've started ...
Hugh Yes—I—

Sven is seen jigging about, preparing to receive service

Richard (*off*) Ready?
Sven Right.
Brian (*off*) Play.

Sven rushes in

Sven (*off*) Ah.
Brian (*off*) Fifteen-love.
Mo (*off*) Hooray, hooray.
Sven (*returning*) I hope that girl isn't going to keep that up all afternoon.
Olive Shhhh ...
Sven Ah.
Brian (*off*) Thirty-love.
Mo Hooray, hooray.
Richard (*off*) Sorry. A bit flukey.
Anthea I'd stand a bit closer to the net, Sven, if I was you. The ball's so wet it hardly travels.

Sven Thank you, Anthea, I know what I'm doing, thank you.

Sven crouches. He runs in

(*off*) Ah-ha!
Brian Thirty-fifteen.
Mo (*off*) Boo.
Richard (*off*) Good shot.

Sven returns pleased. He crouches to receive, runs in.

Hugh Anthea, I—could I—have a word ...
Sven (*off*) Ah.
Brian (*off*) Forty-fifteen.
Mo (*off*) Hooray, hooray, 'ray, 'ray, 'ray ...
Sven Oh, shut up, you rowdy little girl.
Mo Boo. Boo. Boo-boo-boo ...
Sven (*returning indignantly*) How can I concentrate with that—that ...
Olive Be quiet.
Brian (*off*) Shut up, Mo.

Mo shuts up. Sven runs in to meet the service

Sven (*off*) Oh, damn to hell.
Richard (*off*) Bad luck.
Brian (*off*) Game to Richard. One-love.

Sven returns into sight, dejected. Olive follows him from outside the court

Olive How are you feeling, dear?
Sven Olive, you are sorely trying my patience. (*Shouting down to Richard*) Ready?
Richard (*off*) Yes.
Sven (*stepping towards the base line for a mighty serve*) Right.

A grunt as Sven serves, almost immediately the ball flies back hitting the back netting

Brian (*off*) Love-fifteen.
Anthea Oh, good shot.
Hugh Anthea, I think I have to say this now ...
Anthea Oh yes?

Sven serves again

Richard (*off*) Nice one.
Brian (*off*) Fifteen-all.
Anthea Well served. (*To Hugh*) Is it about the Famine Relief envelopes? Because most of those are being done by the W.I.s. I had a word with their chairman, Molly Maintrap, and she's farmed them out to volunteers.

During the above Sven has served successfully again

Brian (*off*) Thirty-fifteen.
Olive Well played, dear.

Anthea Bravo.

Hugh No, it's more than that, you see ...

Anthea (*calling across to Olive*) He's got a jolly good service, hasn't he?

Sven (*appearing in view momentarily*) Of course, I have a jolly good service.

Sven turns, runs in and serves. The ball comes hurtling back

Brian (*off*) Thirty-all.

Sven (*returning to gather the ball, sourly*) Good shot, good shot.

Hugh (*urgently*) Anthea, please.

Anthea Hang on, Hugh love. This is getting very exciting.

Sven serves

Richard (*off*) Hey. No chance ...

Brian (*off*) Forty-thirty.

Mo (*off*) Come on, Richard.

Olive Come on, Sven.

Anthea Come on, Sven.

Sven serves. Richard returns. Sven wins

Brian (*off*) Game to Sven, one-all.

Anthea Well done. Well played. You're looking awfully hang-dog, Hugh. Are you all right?

Hugh No, I'm not all right. That's why I want to talk to you.

Anthea Are you ill?

Hugh I think I am, in a sense.

Sven (*off*) Ah.

Brian (*off*) Fifteen-love.

Richard (*off*) Were you ready?

Sven (*off*) Yes, yes, yes.

Hugh You see, the point is—I—well—you see the ...

Brian (*off*) Fifteen-all.

Anthea Hugh, what are you talking about?

Hugh Do we have to talk here?

Anthea Well, I'm watching the game.

Hugh Yes but—I was going to talk to you in the New Year but ...

Sven (*off*) Ahhh ...

Richard (*off*) Good shot.

Brian (*off*) Fifteen-thirty.

Anthea Come in and have some tea with us afterwards and ...

Hugh No, no.

Sven (*off*) Ah-ha!

Brian (*off*) Fifteen-forty.

Mo (*off*) Come on, Richard.

Anthea Come on, Richard. Poor Hugh, have you had a miserable Christmas?

Hugh Well—fairly ...

Anthea Was Christopher playing up?

Hugh No, he's really much better. He's grown into a very quiet boy. Almost secretive, I suppose. Very contained. I don't think he loves either of us very much...

Richard (*off*) Ahhh ...!

Brian (*off*) Thirty-forty.

Mo (*off*) Hooray.

Hugh Still, things have definitely turned a corner.

Anthea Good shot. And Louise is looking better.

Hugh Yes, well that's very largely thanks to you, Anthea. I mean, you've taken practically all her worries off her shoulders ...

Anthea Oh, rubbish. I've rattled a few collecting tins, that's all.

Hugh And all those leaflets.

Anthea Five minute job.

Hugh And the jumble sales.

Anthea They're enormous fun.

The ball hits the netting

Sven (*following it*) That was out.

Richard (*off*) Oh, well played.

Brian (*off*) Game to Sven. Sven leads two-one.

Sven We're really getting warmed up now.

Richard arrives beside him

(*Startled*) What are you doing?

Richard Aren't we changing ends?

Sven Oh yes. You want to go straight on?

Richard Might as well before it gets dark.

Sven Right. Fit, fit, fit.

Sven sprints off up the other end. Anthea laughs

Richard (*to Anthea*) There's no stopping him. On we go.

Richard positions himself at this end of the court. The game continues under the next with Sven serving from the other end. Eight points in all. The majority of the action takes place off

Olive (*moving away from the court towards the house*) I think I'll fetch him a glass of water. He's looking very hot.

Anthea Oh, fine. You know where ...

Olive Yes. I do hope he wins. I dread to think what he'll be like to live with if he doesn't.

Anthea It's all right. Don't worry. Don't worry.

Olive goes off worried

Hugh Anthea.

Anthea Now, Hugh. Come on then, tell me all about it. Is it another crisis of faith?

Hugh No, no. Well, not really.

Anthea Oh good. Because you know, I'm not good at those. We've solved some pretty knotty ones though, haven't we?

Hugh Yes, well the point is, Anthea, I don't know whether half the problems

I have come to you with are genuine or not. It's not the problems so much as the ... This is not the easiest thing to say at the best of times. Particularly not coming from someone in my position. It's something I shouldn't say. And yet, if I don't say it, maybe the very fact of my not saying it will be just as bad in the long run as if I had said it.

Anthea Said what?

Brian (*off*) Fifteen-love.

Hugh I am in love with you.

A pause

Anthea (*blankly*) What?

Hugh I am in love with you. It happened a very long time ago actually. I think at first, it was just a general sort of love for both of you. You and Richard—as people. I don't know if you're aware of it but you're both very good people. At least I feel you are.

Brian (*off*) Fifteen-all.

Hugh And I think it was that very goodness that I fell in love with. Your unselfishness, your generosity ... You were in a way everything I wanted to be but couldn't be. I almost envied you.

Anthea But, Hugh ...

Hugh Please. Let me say it all first.

Brian (*off*) Thirty-fifteen.

Hugh You can imagine if this has been happening over eight years, then it's pretty permanent as far as I am concerned. In fact it's taken me over completely. It's killed what little there was between Louise and me. It was unfortunate in the first place, marrying a woman I realize I cared for hardly at all. But at least the lack of feeling is mutual at any rate. Whereas my love for you ... I promise you I've tried desperately hard to stop this feeling for you from growing. Or at any rate, tried to channel it into more conventional Christian love ...

Brian (*under the above*) Forty-fifteen.

Hugh (*continuing, but closing his eyes and beginning to speak faster and faster*) But whenever we are together, I feel overwhelmed with a desire for you, a longing for you—not just a spiritual longing, I'm afraid. I pray God it were just a spiritual longing but it's not. It's good old fully-fledged carnal longing as well. For you and your body. For all of you. And I want you and I need you ...

Brian (*off*) Forty-thirty.

Hugh (*continuing remorsely*) And I'm sorry, I'm sorry, I'm sorry, forgive me. I am a middle-aged clergyman who's making a fool of himself and ought to know better but I love you, Anthea, I love you. For ever and ever and ever. World without end.

Brian (*off*) Deuce.

Anthea (*after a pause, in a strangled voice*) Oh, dear God.

Brian (*off*) Advantage Sven.

Hugh Dear God indeed.

Anthea Oh Hugh ....

The ball hits the back fence

Richard (*following it up*) That was in.
Brian (*off*) Game and set to Sven.
Richard Congratulations, Sven mate. Well played.

Olive enters with a glass of water

Olive What happened? Is he all right?
Richard All right? He won.
Olive He won?
Sven (*appearing*) Of course I won.
Olive Oh, well done. Well done. (*to Anthea*) He won.
Anthea Oh good.
Sven Well now, who's for another game?
Richard Not at the moment, thank you.
Sven So perish all enemies of the Finnish Junior Champion.
Olive He hasn't played for ten years either.
Brian (*coming out of the court and patting Sven's shoulder*) Very good. Well
  played.
Sven Yes, I think we must play some more, eh?
Richard The court's there. Any time.
Mo (*coming round the side of the court to Richard*) You bloody twit.
Richard What?
Mo Whyn't you beat him?
Richard They're too good these Finnish Junior Champions.
Mo Rubbish. He's a rubbish player. You can beat him ...
Sven (*coolly ignoring this*) Coming in, my darling? It's a little chilly.
Olive Yes, you mustn't catch a chill.
Mo (*to Richard*) Why didn't you play with your proper hand then?
Richard What?
Mo Why?
Richard Don't know what you mean.
Mo You know.
Sven What is she talking about?
Mo I am asking him why he played you left-handed when he was right-handed
  when he played with us.
Sven You were playing left-handed?
Richard Well.
Sven Against me?
Richard Um ...
Sven But you're right-handed.
Anthea He wasn't, he ...
Mo He was. I watched him. That's why he lost.
Sven You were playing with me left-handed?
Richard Well, some of the time. Thought I'd ring the changes.
Sven I see. I see. At least you paid me the compliment of not hopping on
  one leg as well. Let's go in.

Sven goes off with Olive

Anthea (*after a pause*) I don't think that was awfully clever.
Richard Well—he—I thought he needed to win.
Anthea Yes, but couldn't you have lost right-handed?
Richard Yes, I—oh hell. Too late now, isn't it? Sorry.

Richard goes in dejected

Mo (*muttering*) Twit.
Brian Your husband's going to get himself murdered one of these days.

Brian and Mo go in

Anthea finds herself alone again with Hugh

Anthea Oh Hugh ...

Hugh smiles weakly

Have you ever mentioned this to Louise?
Hugh No, no.
Anthea Well, please never do.
Hugh Oh no–never, never. I wouldn't—it would ... No.
Anthea Oh, Hugh.
Hugh I love you.
Anthea Go home.
Hugh Yes. Quite right. Good night.
Anthea Good night.

Hugh goes. Anthea, after a moment goes in too as—

the CURTAIN *falls*

SCENE 2

The same. Four years later. A summer evening, about 7 p.m.

*Brian and Richard are busy running sound and lights out to the tennis court.
Richard is in the tennis court up a stepladder clamping a floodlight to the rail.
A mains lead runs from the court into the house. Brian enters carrying a
loud-speaker from the house into the tennis court. Sven is sitting in the summer
house watching them at work. Despite the fine evening, he wears a light coat*

Sven (*as Brian appears*) My word, my word. More and more.
Richard Won't be a minute, Sven. This is the last one.
Brian (*with the loud-speaker*) You want this one in the other corner?
Richard I think so, don't you? The lead should reach all right.

Brian goes off to the far end of the court

Sven And all this for little Debbie.
Richard (*wrestling with the lamp*) Yeah.
Sven A very lucky young lady.
Richard Oh well, eighteenth birthday. Quite a milestone.

Sven Eighteen, my goodness.
Richard Are you all right there? Do you want anything?
Sven No, no, no. Olive is fetching me my drink.

Brian appears

Brian Shall I tie those leads against the wire? People are going to trip on them otherwise.
Richard Yes, not too securely. The first sign of rain I've got to whip this lot in. It's rather expensive this gear.

Brian goes

Sven You'll have to hope she has well-behaved friends, young Debbie.
Richard Oh, they're not too bad, the ones we've met. I mean, they scare the life out of me to look at but they're not too badly behaved.
Sven How many are you expecting?
Richard God knows. It started at thirty. I think it's gone up to fifty now. We set the limit at fifty so we're expecting about seventy-five.
Brian (*off*) You want me to test this?
Richard Would you? And could you plug the floods in for a second, too?
Brian (*off*) Okay.
Richard (*coming down the steps and heading towards the house*) Hang on, I'll switch it on at the other end.
Brian (*off*) Righto.

Olive enters from the house with a medicinal concoction

Richard (*nearly colliding with Olive*) Sorry.
Olive It's like a madhouse here.
Richard We'll be straight in a minute.
Olive I nearly fell over that wire back there.
Richard I'm fixing it down, my love.

Richard goes

Olive (*handing Sven the medicinal concoction*) Here we are. Like a madhouse back there.
Sven Is that anything unusual.
Olive Do you want me to bring the car rug to wrap round you?
Sven I'm fine, my darling I'm perfectly capable. Don't treat me like a two year-old.
Olive (*looking at the tennis court*) What are they doing?
Sven They're going to have dancing in the tennis court. There's the lights and the music, you see. Which Brian's fixing.
Olive Oh, I see.

Richard returns

Richard (*calling to Brian*) Anything?
Brian (*off*) Not yet.
Richard See that switch on the plug is on ... No, the one that end. (*Turning to the others*) You looking after him, Olive?

Sven She's looking after me far too much. I'm being ridiculously spoilt.
Olive He won't let me look after him half the time.
Richard You seem better.
Olive If he's sensible and does as he's told, he'll never have any trouble again. That is a fact. The thing about a heart condition is provided you're sensible, it needn't be a worry.
Sven I'm being perfectly sensible. I'm doing absolutely nothing. What less could I do?

The floodlights and other lights come on momentarily

Richard They're working fine.
Brian (*off*) Is that one on by me?
Richard Yes. (*To the others*) It's good you came.
Olive Well, we couldn't miss Debbie's eighteenth, could we? I mean, that's the really important one these days, isn't it? I mean, in our youth it used to be your twenty first but...
Sven Of course the whole legal position has changed now since the voting age was reduced. This has made...
Olive Of course, we've known Debbie since she was, what, three.
Sven This has made ... (*He gives up*)
Olive Is Giles here?
Richard No, he's keeping well away. Staying with a schoolfriend. He has a very low opinion of Debbie's associates.
Olive Oh dear.
Richard He says they're frivolous. Very serious young man is Giles. Not awfully bright but very serious.
Sven Well, he's of an age. Of an age. Don't you remember...

A blast of loud music from the speakers causes him to jump

Oh, my God.
Olive (*rushing to Sven's side*) Oh heavens.
Richard (*simultaneously calling to Brian*) Hey, hey.

The music stops

Brian (*off*) Sorry.
Olive Are you all right?
Sven Yes, yes. Just about. Oh dear, oh dear.
Richard Sorry about that.
Olive You're sure you're all right, dear?
Sven This man is obviously trying to kill me. He takes over the business. He practically sees me into a wheelchair, now he's trying to kill me.
Richard Hardly.
Olive Calm down, now, calm down.
Sven No, I'm joking. I'm joking. But Richard, you must understand that I won't be as active as I was for some time. You understand that?
Olive Yes, he understands that.
Richard You'd better hurry up. The place can't run without you, you know.
Sven No, Richard, please, don't start kindnesses, please. I'm old enough now

to see for myself my strength and my weaknesses. If that hasn't happened to a man by the time he's forty-two years old, then heaven help him. Despite what my darling Olive may say to the contrary, I'm a man of only average ability. An average ability only. Before I reached this shattering conclusion, I once made the mistake, Richard, of trying to compete with you. You responded to my challenge with a gesture of supreme disdain. Playing with me left-handed. Not only in tennis but also in business.

Richard I don't think I did that.

Sven Oh, Richard ... The fact is, when it comes down to it, you have the one advantage over me that matters. You have flair, Richard. That's something that can't be learnt. It's handed out at birth along with all those other unfair advantages like physical beauty under a most monstrously devised random system. And as always happens on these occasions, it always goes to the very people who in my opinion do least to earn it. It's taken me forty-two years to think of that and I'm very depressed.

Olive (*getting tearful*) He goes on like that these days for hours. I don't know. I don't listen.

Richard I don't quite see what I'm supposed to do. Sorry, I ...

Sven Nothing, Richard. Nothing more than usual. Kindly continue to support us all in the style to which we are accustomed, that's all.

Richard (*smiling*) I'll do my best.

Anthea enters with a tray of drinks. It is another concoction in a jug

Anthea (*putting the tray on the table*) Here we are. I thought we'd sample this. Debbie and I concocted it for the party. We can drink her health.

Richard I'd be very wary of that if I were you.

Anthea Are the lights working?

Richard Yes.

Anthea Do they look all right?

Richard Well, yes. A bit like a prisoner-of-war camp but not bad. I've put some colours in. It's made it a little more tasteful.

Anthea Well, don't ruin those lamps. They want them back for *White Horse Inn* next week. (*Pouring out a glass*) Sven won't, will he?

Olive No.

Anthea You will?

Olive Well, a little one. I'm driving.

Anthea Oh lord, so you are. Is it a hell of a hike?

Olive Not too bad.

Sven No, once we get on to the motorway ...

Anthea What's the latest you can leave?

Olive We ought to be away by eight. It's an hour's drive.

Sven Yes, but once we get on to the motorway—

Anthea Well, you'll have time for a quick snack anyway. (*Calling to Brian*) Brian, do you want some of this? (*She pours*)

Sven (*muttering*) —it'll be plain sailing.

Olive What's that, dear? (*She sits by him*)

Sven Nothing, my darling.

Brian appears from the tennis court

Brian Yes, ta. Leave it there for me. Richard, I'll loop these leads up out of the way.
Richard Fine.
Brian (*holding up some wire*) Can I use this wire?
Richard Go ahead.

Brian takes the steps and disappears again

Anthea I'll leave it here. (*She puts the glass on the tray*)
Olive Where's Debbie then?
Anthea (*moving to sit at the table*) Very, very slowly getting out of the bath, when I last saw her. It's lovely you managed to break your journey. Thank you. She really does appreciate it.
Olive Oh well...
Anthea Well, I think she does, anyway...
Olive How do you mean?
Anthea Oh, it's always awkward to know what to do when they get to that age and they're still living at home. I mean, to be truthful, she'd be far happier if we weren't here at all but seeing as it's our house, too bad. So we said to her, right. Ten minutes of boring old us—happy birthday from the older generation and so on and then we'll vanish...
Sven Older generation. Now, we're the older generation.
Olive We're not in the grave yet.
Sven You hear that, Richard? Older generation?
Richard (*moving to Brian*) Yes. Be careful of that speaker wire. It's caught round the net post.
Brian (*off*) Oh yeah.

Richard goes into the court and disappears

Anthea She'll be down in a minute.
Olive Are the—er—are the Emersons coming round?
Anthea Ah. Thereby hangs a tale. Possibly. I've asked them.
Olive Oh, are they...?
Anthea Oh dear. Well, Louise has been—you know, peculiar again. And Hugh had to get her mother in to look after her and then Hugh and her mother had a row and—oh gosh, yes. If they do come, don't whatever you do ask after Christopher.
Olive Something wrong?
Anthea With Christopher? No, he's fine. In fact he's brilliant. I mean, he got this public school scholarship, of course, and now he's got a University Open Scholarship and he's only seventeen. I mean, he's got to be Prime Minister or something, hasn't he?
Olive I should think they're very proud.
Anthea They would be. Only he won't speak to them, that's the trouble. He really is a weird youth when you meet him. You can almost hear his brain going round as he stares at you. Quite spooky. He's completely cut off from Louise and Hugh. He's quite gentle with them. He treats them like a couple of deaf-mute family retainers.

Olive Oh dear.

Anthea It's one of the reasons for Louise's condition, of course. She has her high days and low days, a bit like the church. It depends what miracle drug the doctor's currently got her on. She can get anything from soporific to suicidal. We haven't seen them for yonks. We asked them today, of course. Well, it wouldn't be the same without them, would it?

Richard (*off*) That's it. Pull the whole thing this way a bit.

Brian (*off*) Okay.

Sven (*who has been watching the men during this last, muttering*) No, no, no. You'll never do it if you pull it that way. You'll never do it ...

Richard (*off*) That's it. That's done it.

Brian Thank you. Brilliant.

Sven (*muttering*) Oh, well, I don't know ...

Anthea Have you got a nice hotel?

Olive Yes. Well, it looks nice in the pictures. It's a ...

Sven Four star. English catering. Hard beds. No air conditioning. If you put your shoes outside to be cleaned, they're stolen in the night. It'll be hell on earth. But who cares, we're on holiday.

Olive It looked very nice.

Anthea You should have stayed here.

Richard wanders back from the tennis court

Olive Oh no.

Anthea We'd've looked after you.

Sven No, no, no.

Anthea Wouldn't we, Richard? They should have stayed here with us. We'd've built you up.

Olive Oh yes. We can do without that. It's all right for you. Look at you.

Anthea (*rising*) Look, I can call now and cancel.

Olive (*rising*) Oh no, it's ...

Sven No, Anthea. Please.

Anthea Well, it's silly. You can have all the rest in the world here. Don't you agree, Richard?

Richard No, Antie.

Anthea But it's stupid.

Richard Antie, I think they want to go to the hotel.

Anthea But it makes no sense.

Richard Antie, don't push them, darling.

Anthea I'm not, I—oh, well, super. Fine. I mean, suit yourself.

Olive Be best. (*She sits*)

Hugh and Louise appear round the side of the tennis court: Hugh, pale and drawn; Louise, bright, like a painted doll. She is smiling incessantly, but unnaturally, as one under the influence of drugs. She is, in fact, under the influence of drugs

Richard Hallo, there.

Anthea Oh, splendid. Welcome. Come on.

Hugh Hallo.

Louise (*chirpily*) Hallo.
Olive Hallo. Lovely to see you both. Been a long time.
Louise Hallo.
Hugh Yes, yes. Over a year, I think, at least.
Louise (*to Sven*) Hallo. (*She sits at the table*)
Olive It must be. Of course, Sven's illness has meant ...
Hugh Yes, of course. How are you, Sven? Are you better? You look good.
Sven Yes, I'm well mended now, Hugh.
Hugh You look good.
Sven Yes, I'm well mended.
Hugh Yes, you look good.
Sven Yes.
Hugh Good, good.
Louise Hallo, Richard.
Sven Excuse me, Louise, if I don't bound up to greet you in my customary manner but I'm not allowed too much violent exercise.
Hugh No more games of tennis then, eh?
Sven No, no. No more games of tennis.

A pause. Louise rises

Louise (*seeing Brian*) Hallo. (*She sits*)
Brian (*off*) Hallo.
Anthea You're looking very bright, Louise.
Louise Yes, yes.
Hugh She's on these new stimulants. I think they're rather stronger than she's used to. But we're giving them a try.
Louise Yes.
Richard Is she allowed a glass of ... (*He indicates the tray*)
Louise Oh, super.
Hugh No, not with these particular pills. They would react, dear.
Richard Oh dear. A small glass for you?
Hugh Thank you, Richard. A very small glass.

Anthea pours Hugh a glass

Hugh Yes, well, good health. And—um--where's the girl of the moment?
Anthea She's coming down. She takes hours over everything these days. She's been getting ready since this morning.
Hugh Oh well, after all, that's ... that's—er ... that's—er ... er ... that's ...
Richard Youth.
Hugh Yes. Youth, yes.

A pause

Louise (*laughing suddenly*) This is fun, isn't it?
Anthea Yes, yes.

A pause

Hugh (*confidentially*) Er, I thought we'd check first—er—we didn't quite know what to give her ...

Anthea Oh no, no. For heaven's sake, don't give her anything. She's most horribly spoilt.

Hugh (*producing a small, badly wrapped parcel*) Yes, well—it's a bit—a bit obvious but—I wondered if she'd like this ... if not, I could probably get her something else—but—er—you see—quickly, have a look. (*Showing Anthea*) It's a cross, you see. It belonged to my grandmother, actually.

Anthea Oh Hugh, it's lovely.

Hugh It's not at all valuable or anything.

Anthea It's beautiful. Look, Richard.

Richard (*approvingly*) Lovely.

Hugh Do you think she might...

Anthea Oh, she'd adore it. She loves anything like this, doesn't she, Richard?

Richard Are you sure you want to give it away, Hugh?

Hugh Oh yes, yes.

Richard I mean, wouldn't Louise like it?

Hugh No, Louise wanted her to have it.

Louise Yes, she must have it. She must have it. Debbie must have it.

Anthea Well, it's glorious. She'll love it.

A slight pause.

Sven and Olive gave her a record token.

Hugh Ah-ha.

Olive It was quite a big record token.

Hugh Yes. Well, that's probably something much nearer to her heart if we did but know it.

Another pause.

Louise (*laughing again*) Really fun, isn't it?

Anthea Look, I'm going to see where Debbie's got to. Her friends are going to start arriving soon and Sven and Olive have got a journey and, well, we've all got things to do, haven't we? Won't be a sec.

Anthea goes

A silence

Richard Brian, come and have a glass of this.

Brian appears in the tennis court

Brian (*coming out of the tennis court*) All right, thanks. (*Sensing the atmosphere*) Thank you. (*He takes his glass*)

Hugh (*indicating the tennis court*) And that's where it's all happening, is it?

Brian Oh yes, yes. Just been rigging up the sound.

Richard Now, remember, if it gets too much for you, let us know. We won't let them go on too late.

Hugh Oh, a little bit of music—do us good, eh? (*He smiles at Louise*)

Louise Yes.

Richard I'll cut them off at the mains if it gets too much.

Hugh Well, don't worry on our account.

Sven Young people, eh?
Hugh Yes.
Sven If you have children, you must expect to pay the penalty.
Hugh (*clouding*) Yes—yes...

A pause

Sven Yes, yes, yes. (*To Olive*) Remember that hotel? They actually stole my
   shoes.
Olive Yes, dear.
Hugh Oh.

A pause. Louise starts singing softly

Louise If you—(*singing*)—go down to the woods today...

Hugh looks apprehensive

   *Before anyone can really react, Anthea enters, ushering in Debbie, her
   eighteen-year-old daughter: a pleasantly "normal" girl with a great deal of
   Anthea's straight-forwardness about her; though, being younger, in older company she is at present understandably shy*

Anthea Eureka.
Richard Oh, I don't believe it.
Olive Ah, there she is.
Louise Hallo, Debbie.
Sven Debbie, my dear.
Hugh Hallo.
Sven Look at the child. Look at the dear child, how she grows.
Debbie Hallo.
Brian (*offering a drink*) Debbie, will you?
Debbie Thank you, Uncle Brian ... (*Confused*) I mean, Brian. I'm sorry.
Brian (*embarrassed*) I made her promise not to call me Uncle Brian now she's
   eighteen.
Olive Yes, well. Makes you feel your age.
Sven I'm sorry I can't bound up to greet you, Debbie, in my customary fashion
   but, you know, we old men, eh?
Debbie Thank you very much for the token.
Sven Well...
Olive A little something.

Pause

Anthea Well, look, darling, we're not going to embarrass you any more.
   Heaven knows why we're doing this really. I suppose it's because we're all
   people who are very fond of you and we wanted, on your birthday, to say
   it to you personally. Just quickly. So, you know I'm awful at speeches, but
   I'm sorry if we're being a drag for you. Happy birthday, darling, that's
   all. And may you have many happy ones to come.
Louise Hear, hear.
Richard Hear, hear. (*Raising his glass*) To you, Debbie. Happy birthday.

Olive ⎫
Hugh ⎬ Happy birthday, Debbie. ⎫ *Speaking*
Brian ⎭   ⎬ *together*
                                         ⎭

They are about to drink

Sven Sorry, Anthea—may I just...? Excuse me, Richard. Debbie, I just wanted to add a word, if I may. I wish you success, Debbie. I know you will have success because you come from a family which knows nothing but success. There are some lucky ones among us who we refer to as being born with a silver spoon in their mouths. You, Debbie, have been born with a whole canteen of cutlery. May I, on behalf of life's losers, those of us without a lousy plastic teaspoon to our name, ask you, please to accept humble greetings from one middle-aged mediocrity...

Olive starts crying

Shut up, Olive—who has fought and lost. Remember if you will, Debbie, this saying: The tragedy of life is not that man loses but that he almost wins.

A silence except for Olive's sobs. Sven shrugs, a man exhausted. His chin drops on his chest

Debbie (*totally stunned*) Thank you.
Anthea (*softly*) Olive, dear.

Louise laughs for no good reason

Hugh (*moving forward tentatively*) Debbie, we thought perhaps you'd care to ... We thought perhaps you might like...

Hugh offers the present. Debbie accepts

Debbie Oh, thank you. (*She holds it*) Thank you very much.
Louise Open it up, Debbie.
Anthea (*prompting*) Open it.
Debbie All right.

Debbie opens the present

Louise Isn't it gorgeous?
Debbie Yes. Thank you. Very much.
Anthea Aren't you lucky?
Hugh (*clearing his throat*) We felt that that little gift, Debbie, would help to remind you in the days ahead ... when you walk in the paths, that ... nevertheless, in that, you will find a reminder of all the good things in life. That are important. I think they're important anyway and I'm sure you do. And that you will remember and treasure it always in your heart. I think, Debbie, that you could do a lot worse than hold up your mother ... in your eyes, as it were, as someone very much to live by, as is your father too, in a different way. I think, knowing these wonderful people as I do, you should be very proud. (*He steps back*)
Anthea Thank you, Hugh.

Debbie looks totally baffled

Debbie Thank you.

Louise starts to sing the hymn, "Glorious things of thee are spoken..." They stare at her. She invites them to join in

Hugh Louise...
Richard (*briskly*) Well, I think that's as good a cue as any for us all to buzz off and leave you to your party, Debbie.
Anthea Yes, quite right. Look at the time. We've got to feed them all and put them on the road. Olive, would you...
Olive (*blowing her nose and helping Sven to rise*) Yes.

Louise sings on. Olive and Sven move to the path to the house

Anthea Hugh?
Hugh (*apologetically*) I am sorry. She's—we're changing the prescription on Monday.
Anthea That's quite all right. I think it's rather jolly.
Hugh It is in short bursts, but she can go on indefinitely. She falls asleep singing.
Anthea It's like Christmas.
Hugh Anthea, I must talk to you urgently.
Anthea Yes, all right, Hugh. Later, later. In you go.

Anthea ushers Hugh and Louise along

Olive (*passing Debbie, gripping her arm*) God bless you, Debbie.
Debbie Thank you.
Sven I won't wish you good luck, Debbie. It's people like us who need good luck.

Sven and Olive go out

Louise Bye-bye, Debbie.
Debbie Good-bye.
Hugh Good-bye, Debbie.
Debbie Thank you. Good-bye.
Louise Bye-bye.

Hugh and Louise go out

Brian Shall I switch things on, now?
Richard Oh, would you, Brian? Thanks. We'll set everything working for you, Debbie.
Brian (*going into the court*) Shall I put on some music?
Richard Yes, not too loud. Not till the Holmensons are on their way.

Richard gathers up the glasses.

Brian goes out of sight

Anthea goes to Debbie

Anthea Well done, darling. You coped very well with all that. Very tactful.
Debbie Haven't you got any normal friends at all?
Anthea What on earth do you mean?

Debbie Well, they're sort of lost-looking.
Anthea I don't think you could call them—not really. You see, I've always said this to you, Debbie, some of us are very lucky. We have everything we want. We've got enough money. We've got people we love round us all the time and it's easy enough to forget those who haven't. But I think it really is up to us who have to help the others a little bit.
Richard You think it might be worth opening that champagne?
Anthea There's a thought.
Richard Might just cheer things up a bit.
Anthea Well, I could do with it.
Richard Right. (*He moves towards the house*)
Anthea Don't forget the pie.
Richard Under control.
Anthea And there's some fresh baked bread on the top.
Richard Right. (*Kissing Debbie in passing*) Happy birthday, darling.
Debbie Thank you. (*She kisses him*)
Richard (*going*) Be good.

Richard goes into the house

Soft music from the speakers in the tennis court

(*As he goes*) That sounds good.
Anthea Lovely. Are you going to do the lights, Brian?
Brian (*off*) Yes.
Anthea (*confidentially to Debbie*) Darling...
Debbie Mmm?
Anthea Could you try and be specially nice to Brian while he's here this time?
Debbie How do you mean?
Anthea Well, don't tease him about his age, like you do. I mean, Richard and I don't mind but Brian's rather sensitive.
Debbie Oh well, he asks for it. He dyes his hair, did you know?
Anthea Well, he's got no-one at the moment and so he's rather lonely.
Debbie What are you suggesting? I'm not getting that close. He's terribly creepy.
Anthea Now, Debbie, he's perfectly harmless.
Debbie He is not harmless.
Anthea Nonsense, of course he is.
Debbie What about all these girls he brings down?
Anthea Ssh.
Debbie Well.
Anthea He never does anything with them.

The lights go on.

Oh, lovely!
Debbie How do you know?
Anthea Because I know Brian. My God, darling, I was only just a bit older than you when I shared a room with him for three months. Nothing happened. Nothing.

Debbie Gosh. Do you think he's...
Anthea No, he's a nothing. He's a neutral. All I'm saying is be pleasant.

Brian emerges from the tennis court

Doesn't that all look splendid? I must see to people. Have a lovely party,
darling. (*She kisses Debbie*)
Debbie Thank you. (*She kisses Anthea*) Oh, Ma... (*She hands her the cross*)
Anthea (*as she goes*) If you're still dancing at dawn, I'll join you.

Anthea goes

Brian and Debbie stand

Brian Well. Anything else I can do?
Debbie No. (*Pause*) No, I can't think of anything.
Brian Right. Well, have a good party.
Debbie Thank you.
Brian (*about to say something else*) Well, I'll—go in...
Debbie Yes.

Brian moves towards the house

Er...
Brian (*stopping and turning*) Yes?
Debbie Oh nothing. Good night.
Brian 'Night.

Brian goes into the house

Debbie watches him go

Debbie (*to herself, wrinkling her face in disgust*) Uggh. Sorry. Not even for
Mummy.

*Debbie dances by herself to the music while waiting for her guests to arrive,
as—*

the CURTAIN *falls*

FURNITURE AND PROPERTY LIST

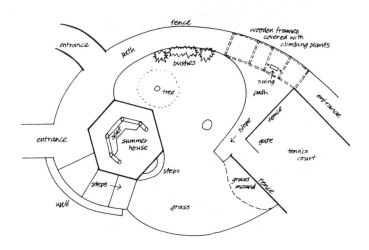

ACT I

SCENE 1

On stage: Summerhouse with fixed seat
Tree stump
Tree (bare)
Bushes (bare)
Rough grass and mound
Part of tennis court with high wire fence
One or two toys, for small children, as dressing

Off stage: Battery lantern (**Richard**)
Small pocket torch (**Anthea**)
Box of matches (**Richard**)
Tray with jug of soup, 8 mugs, dish of hot sausages (**Brian**)
Piece of timber (**Richard**)

Personal: **Sven:** wristwatch

Scene 2

Strike: Bare tree and bushes
Trays, mugs, food
Toys

Set: Tree in leaf
        Bushes in leaf
        Toys, as dressing, for older children: scooter, large rag doll, etc.
        Tennis balls in court
        Rackets (for **Brian** and **Richard**) in court
        Sketch block, pencils on bank (for **Mandy**)
        Wicker table & 3 chairs in summerhouse
        Brian's sweater in tennis court

Off stage: Pile of Sunday newspapers (**Anthea**)
        2 croquet mallets (**Brian**)
        Croquet ball (**Stage Management**)
        Tray with fruit cup, 8 glasses (**Richard**)

Personal: **Sven:** polaroid glasses
        Hugh: handkerchief bandage

ACT II
SCENE 1

Strike: Tree and bushes in leaf
        Any remaining balls
        Sunday newspapers
        Any remaining glasses
        Torn pieces of drawing
        Chairs and table

Set: Bare tree and bushes
        Glider in summerhouse roof (fixed)
        Various games and older toys—e.g. football
        4 tennis rackets in court (**Mo, Richard, Brian, Anthea**)
        Tennis balls in court
        Richard's jacket in court

Off stage: Glass of water (**Olive**)

Personal: **Brian:** coin

SCENE 2

Strike: Bare tree and bushes
        Tennis balls, rackets
        Glider
        Toys and games
        Glass of water
        Richard's jacket

Set: Trees and bushes in leaf
        Chairs and table as before, with tablecloth
        Table (UC) with food for party, covered with cloth
        Strings of coloured lights and floods along tennis court, with cables
            leading off
        Stepladder in court

Off stage: Twin loudspeakers (**Brian**)
        Glass of medicine (**Olive**)
        Tray with jug of fruit drink and 7 glasses

Personal: **Hugh:** small silver cross wrapped in tissue paper

LIGHTING PLOT

Property fittings required: nil

Exterior. A garden. The same scene throughout

ACT I Scene 1 Night

To open: General effect of fine, clear winter night with a little moon

Cue 1:	**Richard/Anthea:** "Brian!" *Distant firework*	(Page 2)
Cue: 2:	**Hugh:** "... little girl and boy, won't you?" *Distant firework*	(Page 3)
Cue 3:	**Anthea:** "Right" *Firework*	(Page 3)
Cue 4:	**Hugh:** "... got any bangers, Louise" *Firework*	(Page 4)
Cue 5:	**Anthea:** "... matter that much" *Firework*	(Page 4)
Cue 6:	**Anthea:** "... all clear now" *Flash*	(Page 4)
Cue 7:	**Anthea:** "Did you know that ..." *Firework overhead*	(Page 4)
Cue 8:	**Richard** (*off*): "Sorry" *Flash on summerhouse roof*	(Page 4)
Cue 9:	**Brian:** "... heating the soup" *Firework*	(Page 5)
Cue 10:	**Louise:** "... up in the country" *Firework*	(Page 5)
Cue 11:	**Anthea:** "No, no, quite." *Rocket goes up*	(Page 6)
Cue 12:	**Hugh:** "Ah" *Distant rocket explosion*	(Page 6)
Cue 13:	**Brian:** "Something like that" *Rocket goes up, explodes*	(Page 6)
Cue 14:	**Louise:** "... full of good ideas" *Intense white firework*	(Page 6)
Cue 15:	**Brian:** "Yes" *Bonfire lights up*	(Page 8)
Cue 16:	**Anthea:** "Do be your age, Brian" *Distant firework*	(Page 9)
Cue 17:	**Melody:** "... about my problems" *Distant firework*	(Page 10)

Cue 18:	**Hugh:** "Thank you" *Distant firework*	(Page 10)
Cue 19:	**Richard:** "It's very relaxing" *Distant firework*	(Page 11)
Cue 20:	**Anthea:** "I'm joking" *Distant firework*	(Page 11)
Cue 21:	**Hugh:** "Well, yes" *Distant firework*	(Page 11)
Cue 22:	**Anthea** exits *Slow fade down of bonfire*	(Page 16)

ACT I SCENE 2   Day

To open: General effect of warm summer morning
No cues

ACT II SCENE 1   Day

To open: General effect of rainy, grey winter afternoon

| *Cue* 23: | As **Sven/Richard** match begins
Start slow fade towards dusk | (Page 39) |
| *Cue* 24: | **Richard** goes in, dejected
Accelerate light fade | (Page 46) |

ACT II SCENE 2   Evening

To open: General effect of warm summer evening light

Cue 25:	**Sven:** "What less could I do?" *Floods and lights come on momentarily*	(Page 48)
Cue 26:	**Richard:** "Yes" *Lights off*	(Page 48)
Cue 27:	**Debbie** enters *Start slow fade to sunset glow*	(Page 54)
Cue 28:	**Anthea:** "He never does anything with them" *Floods and coloured lights on*	(Page 57)

EFFECTS PLOT

ACT 1

SCENE 1

NOTE:	In general during Scene 1, recorded children's voices are raised as fireworks go off	
Cue 1:	**As CURTAIN rises** *Children's voices from tennis court: fade as action starts*	(Page 1)
Cue 2:	**Richard/Anthea:** "Brian!" *Distant firework*	(Page 3)
Cue 3:	**Louise:** "... for ten minutes" *Children fighting*	(Page 3)
Cue 4:	**Hugh:** "... little girl and boy, won't you" *Distant firework*	(Page 3)
Cue 5:	**Anthea:** "Right" *Firework*	(Page 3)
Cue 6:	**Hugh:** "... got any bangers, Louise" *Firework, and children's cries*	(Page 4)
Cue 7:	**Anthea:** "... matter that much" *Firework*	(Page 4)
Cue 8:	**Anthea:** "... all clear now" *Banger goes off*	(Page 4)
Cue 9:	**Anthea:** "Did you know that ..." *Firework screams overhead*	(Page 4)
Cue 10:	**Richard:** "Sorry" *Children's voices*	(Page 4)
Cue 11:	**Hugh** (*off*): "Quieten down, dear" *Fade down children's voices*	(Page 5)
Cue 12:	**Brian:** "... heating the soup" *Firework*	(Page 5)
Cue 13:	**Louise:** "... up in the country" *Firework*	(Page 5)
Cue 14:	**Anthea:** "No, no, quite" *Swoosh of rocket*	(Page 5)
Cue 15:	**Hugh:** "Ah" *Rocket explosion*	(Page 6)
Cue 16:	**Brian:** "Something like that" *Rocket goes up, explodes*	(Page 6)
Cue 17:	**Louise:** "... full of good ideas" *Firework*	(Page 6)

ACT II
SCENE 1

No cues

SCENE 2

MADE AND PRINTED IN GREAT BRITAIN BY
LATIMER TREND & COMPANY LTD PLYMOUTH
MADE IN ENGLAND